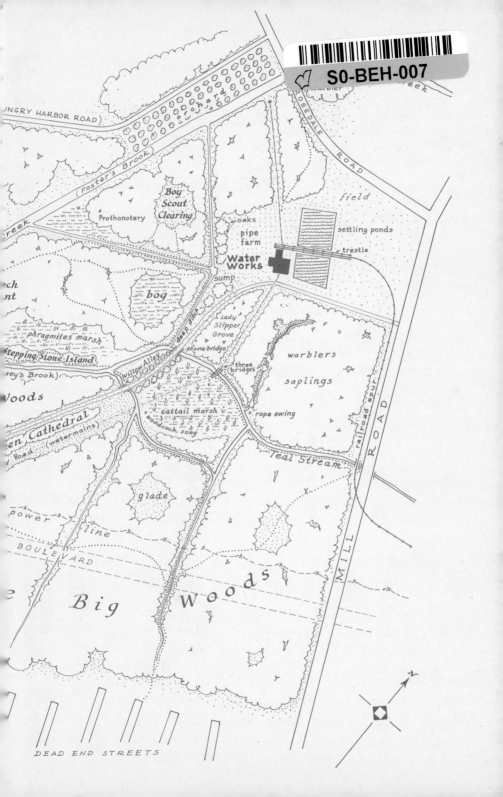

(HUNGRY HARBOR ROAD)

orchard

(Foster's Brook)

ROSEDALE ROAD

warbler

Creek

Creek

Prothonotary

Boy Scout Clearing

field

oaks

pipe farm

Water Works

settling ponds

trestle

sump

bog

deep hole

Lady Slipper Grove

phragmites marsh

stone bridge

three bridges

warblers

saplings

Stepping Stone Island

(xey's Brook)

Willow Alley

Woods

cattail marsh

woodcock song

rope swing

en Cathedral

Road (watermains)

Teal Stream

railroad spur

MILL ROAD

glade

power line

BOULEVARD

Big Woods

DEAD END STREETS

# The Lord's Woods

by Robert Arbib

W · W · Norton & Company · Inc ·
NEW YORK

# The Lord's Woods

For Dave and his boys

# Contents

# Contents

# Foreword

*Whose woods these are I think I know.*
*His house is in the village though;*
*He will not see me stopping here*
*To watch his woods fill up with snow.* *

Whose woods these are I do not know. I have never seen the man or heard his name. But whoever he may be, he is my mortal enemy. By right of title, deed, grant, or fee, or any measure of quiritarian ownership these woods belong to him. It matters not that he is a distant and uninterested proprietor, he is the legal possessor of these acres nonetheless. I see the torn and faded caveats his watchmen posted long ago along his boundaries, and I ignore them. Unafraid I walk the green paths that connect his wells. The smoke from the stack of his pump house flaps down across his snowy fief in sullen folds, and I curse this gray flag of disgrace. By every measure of law and logic, he is the rightful landlord and I the tresspasser.

But I defy him! Put up signs, fences, barricades, come at me with hounds or guns or processes of law. He cannot keep me out or drive me off. For these are not his woods but mine.

* From "Stopping by Woods on a Snowy Evening" from THE POETRY OF ROBERT FROST edited by Edward Connery Lathem. Copyright 1923 by Holt, Rinehart and Winston, Inc. Copyright 1951 by Robert Frost. Reprinted by permission of Holt, Rinehart and Winston, Inc.

11

# Foreword

These woods I walk are mine by right of discovery and by conquest, by patient and private mastery and investiture, inch by inch, pace by pace, in every day and month and season. Mine by right of a thirty-year intimacy and half a lifetime of communion. Only for me and a few others in these times do these woods exist in all their myriad realities and illusions, their lights and shadows, their music and their silences. They are my woods because I am their witness, their guardian, their penitent, and their lover.

These woods are mine in a thousand scenes of grace that are indelible, in a hundred dreams of sun-drenched days and murmuring nights, in memories of the shape and form and texture and scent of each tree and almost every leaf, in every light and every season, and in the echoings of bird songs that shall never be stilled. Down through the years, since the first hour I dared defiance of his privacy, these woods have been a steadfast pivot of my soul; to measure the year by the ebb and flow of life in them, to sense the temper of the times by what was done to them, around them, and over them; to return and rediscover them joyously when I have been far and long away, to remember and draw strength and solace from them when I could not return.

So long as these woods live for me to roam in body or in spirit, so long as the jewelweed hangs heavy in August on the stream banks and autumn whispers with the rustle of bracken-brown thrush, my spirit shall have a secret wellspring, my heart shall have a home, and my America a beloved countenance. But when that dread day comes that has been threatened for so long, when these woods have been allowed to perish through neglect or destroyed for greed, then my spirit shall be dispossessed and I (and you) for all eternity bereft. And because that time seems near at hand, and the long vigil ended, and because the thousands of years that have witnessed their beauty grow and evolve now approach a final agony, I will write this personal memorial. For myself I write it, and for you, to keep the Lord's Woods alive and green forever on these pages and in our hearts.

Then at last, and too late, the trespasser will indeed become the final possessor.

Robert Arbib

# The Lord's Woods

# ONE

# The Discoverers

I WAS NINE years old that June afternoon so many years ago when we first discovered the Lord's Woods, and the world was unspoiled and filled with mysteries. My first two-wheeler, dark red and fast, had come with my birthday in March, and ever since that glorious day my world had been expanding. Only yesterday I had ventured beyond the edge of my universe, out where Westwood Road ceased to be paved and wound into the endless green unknown of the forest. I entered the shadowed stillness of the wilderness in trepidation and in wonder, stopping to dismount at the first bend in the road, peering down the long green tunnel that lay ahead, wondering where, if ever, it ended; whether these woods might go on and on, straight through to Kentucky or perhaps even to Pennsylvania. Then pedaled home at full tilt to find Carl and plan an expedition. Explorers needed companions.

Carl was two years older and taller than I and he lived in the house around the corner; our back yards were separated by a fence now covered with honeysuckle and a gate under the pear tree we could step through or vault over. We were fellow explorers and scientists. Carl was a collector of rare plants and I was gathering the beginnings of a natural history museum in a tiny unused room on our top floor.

# The Lord's Woods

We agreed to an expedition to—and through—the woods the next afternoon, right after Carl's clarinet lesson.

The intrepid explorers set out on foot (no bona fide adventurers ever discovered anything on bicycles) that afternoon, walking through ordinary streets like our own, shaded avenues with wide-spaced houses and their familiar dogs and kids we knew saying *hi*, never suspecting that we were headed straight for Eldorado. We angled across the fields behind the Upper School with all those new brick houses in a row facing them. I had watched them being built the previous summer, had climbed into every one of them when they were still wooden skeletons, had chucked bricks down into the muddy pools in the cellars, had scrambled up ladders to the attics and surveyed the far horizon through window openings high above the surrounding fields. One of the houses even had my initials, B. A. for Bobby Arbib, in the cement in a corner of a cellar floor, where it would remain an enigma for a thousand years. Now these houses were all completed and occupied and closed up like the hostile faces of strangers.

Half a lifetime ago, when I was five, there were no houses anywhere around here; it was all endless meadows. We used to come and fly kites. I would (with help) run the kite into the sky and then flop in the tall grass clutching the tugging string, while crickets trilled all around my head. The fields, now white with oxeye daisies, still reminded me of kites and crickets.

The sidewalk and the paved road came to an abrupt end beyond the last brick house. Here we stepped out of the shimmering sunlight and the reassuring world of houses and school and streets and people into the cool darkness and silence of the forest. Now we were intruders in a place that belonged to someone else, or to no one, and suddenly were were very far from home. We searched for and found two stout sticks to defend ourselves against any sudden attacker we might encounter in this alien world. Explorers always carried weapons.

The road was now a dark gray cinder track and it curved around to the left, past a high, old-fashioned clapboard house dimly seen through the trees. But I had been that way yesterday

16

and remembered a deep-voiced dog and a man who came out onto the veranda and watched silently as I biked bravely into the woods. So we avoided, after consultation, the curving road and found a footpath that plunged straight ahead. No one had been this way today, for the path was hung with spider webs. Unless you were careful you would get a clinging faceful. We knocked down some webs with our staves, but I ducked under one of them. It was too perfect to destroy, with a shiny yellow-and-black demon clinging to its heart. Then Carl walked smack into it.

We hopped across a narrow rivulet, beat through a thicket, and burst out again on the cinder road, now safely past the white farmhouse. The road led straight on into the deepening woods. High overhead the leaves of the canopy were black against the sun, but when you looked down the road, it was a green tunnel with golden light at the far end. It was a mile down to the light, I ventured. But Carl said it was no more than half a mile.

We stood looking down the road, filling our nostrils with the cool, damp air under the trees. The woods were filled with fragrance. Spicy, aromatic foliage smells were mixed with leaf-mold smells, like cinnamon and cloves and nutmeg and all the other sensuous pungencies that filled our kitchen when Eliza was baking. A green smell, I said.

Carl said I was crazy. How could something you couldn't see have a color? But I knew that everything that smelled at all had its special color. In the dark my old brown army blanket smelled blue, not brown at all. Old Mr. Wheeler down the street smelled blue, too. Like a penny, or a nail. Carl thought it was dumb. But to me, even sounds or letters came furnished with colors. One morning last year in third grade I told Miss Wilson that the letter *S* was blue. She asked me whether other letters had colors too. I told her that *A* was yellowy brown. (In *cat*, though, it was yellow.) *I* was silver. *O* was white, of course. *U* was gray. Everybody was laughing. Miss Wilson thought I was goofy. She didn't say so, but she stared at me for a long time and then turned her back to the class. I think she was crying, and I was sorry. (Even with my eyes closed, the woods smelled green, and always would.)

# The Lord's Woods

Now the forest enfolded us, hiding us, dark and deep. Here and there the sun came slanting down through holes, like that spotlight at the Columbia Playhouse, fingering down over our heads to the stage, with dust sparks floating in it. Here there was no stage, no Rockaway Minstrels. Just a shaft of sunlight with one fat bumblebee spinning around and around. Bumble, bumble, bumblebee. Sizzling around in the sunshine. Hey, gee, it was almost summer; school would be over next week!

It was quiet here in the woods, but not if you stopped and listened. If you stood still, you were aware of a constant sound, a hum, a shrill, high-pitched keening. It was bugs, of course, millions of them, singing in their secret homes. Invisible, in the green. In the grass. In the trees, everywhere around us. So persistent, so pervasive, that it seemed to be the sound of summer, the very sound of life itself. At night I could hear it from my bedroom windows, a pulsing, throbbing, never-ending threnody. It had been calling me for years.

Then suddenly we made our first startling discovery. There by a high-banked stream not far from the road stood a strangely deformed tree! Its trunk grew vertically for only a foot or two, then bent horizontally for five or six feet more, then rose vertically again. We ran over and climbed around it, finding cryptic marks on the upper trunk. Carl, who knew about such things, was excited. He said it was an ancient Indian tree, bent as a sapling years ago to mark a trail! A thrill shook me. I peered into the impenetrable brush around us and suddenly there were feathered savages crouching there, silent, motionless. Every leaf that stirred might betray the presence of an Indian brave, with arrow fitted and bow drawn, ready for the sudden swish that killed. I shivered in a momentary breath of icy air. (One day last summer on a Sunday walk my father had shown me a curious stone monument in a little park, dedicated to an Indian chief, and placed there, it said by a white man who had known him many years earlier. That very chief, I was certain, had bent this tree!)

Carl thought the tree was older than that—the oldest object we had ever found. Not as ancient as those dinosaur skeletons that had awed and haunted us in the museum this winter, but still an incredible treasured message from the distant past, when the world was wild and unexplored. We considered racing home for spades and digging under the tree, to find an Indian buried there. A squaw or brave perhaps with a stone tomahawk still imbedded in its skull. Walk into fourth grade Monday with a dirty old skull with a tomahawk stuck in it. Suzanne and Helene and Carolyn would scream. Miss Sheard would have a fit. Better still, I could trade it for a hundred immies or maybe even Kibby's World War hand grenade. But I wouldn't. It would have an honored place in my museum, alongside the carved African war canoe, the wasp nest, the meteorite I had found on Central Avenue (identified years later as a fine specimen of ordinary hematite), and the coral from Bermuda.

But already I had secret misgivings, reflecting on the rightful owner of the skull and how guilty I would feel separating it from the rest of his mortal remains. I would like to find a tomahawk, but not one imbedded in a skull.

We looked down then at the water and saw, riding the mirror of the surface, curious little spiders kicking around, as if on ice. Skating there, hitching themselves across the water in quick spurts, then drifting slowly on the current. Making little dimples in the surface with their feet. Miraculous! We kneeled down and tried to catch one, failed, decided they were not spiders at all (not enough legs), agreed to call them waterwalkers and the bent tree forever afterward the Indian Tree, a secret rendezvous. Then first Carl and then I sealed the pact by trying to drown the waterwalkers with our own waterfalls, and failing that, walked down the cinder road, leaving two nests of golden bubbles to float down the stream behind us.

There was a barrier across the road just ahead: an enormous, rusty iron pipe, half sunk into the ground, as wide as the road and higher than my knees. To keep automobiles out, we agreed. We scrambled over it, teetered along it, peered and hollered through it, and walked on, into the deepening forest. Now in every direction stretched woodland without end. The white farmhouse and the Indian Tree were far behind us, out of sight.

# The Lord's Woods

We were alone in the wilderness. The woods were like an ocean with no limits and no horizon, and we were walking along the dim, silent bottom of it. Just the two of us, alone. With sinister things whispering, twigs unaccountably snapping, and leaves shaking suddenly for no apparent reasons.

"What would you do," I asked Carl, "if someone came along now and chased us?" Did these woods belong to anyone? Could we be arrested for being in here? I thought I would squnch down behind a big tree, hidden in the ferns, and wait until dark to run home. Carl didn't believe that I could be quiet that long. (I didn't either.) I saw the darkness gathering now in the forest; it would be inky black in here at night. I might never find my way out. I shivered again. We walked on.

Something exploded in a treetop above us. "What was that!" I yelped. Nothing but a crazy long-legged bird that jumped out of the crown of the tree and flapped away. There went another, and three more. "And, hey, did you see what he did when he went *quock?* He pooped. In the air!" It was funny, how you couldn't see them until they jumped up and wheeled away. Carl accused me of having jumped too. I denied it loudly, but I knew that deep down I was wary in this lonely, disquieting place. A strange, wild, beautiful place, filled with startling surprises.

Now the woods on both sides and below the cinder road had standing pools of water. One of the maples had fallen over, heaving up its roots in a great mass, leaving a watery hollow in their place. I climbed up to survey the forest, but the perch was precarious, with a foothold and handhold for one. Carl jumped up after me, and we struggled for a moment before I tumbled, landing on my knees in the black pool. "Aw, gee," I protested. "Look what you made me do! My knickers are black and my shoes are filled with water. Oh, well," I consoled myself, "At least I didn't lose my scout knife and the licorice ropes. Gee, that was funny, falling flop off that tree!"

Ferns everywhere around us now, shoulder high, in pale green waves. When Carl walked through the ferns beside the road, it was a disembodied boy's head bouncing along the top of green surf. The ferns smelled strong, like our oriental brass water pitcher at home. Brassy, not green.

A fat, brown bird with a long beak rocketed from the ground at my feet with a whirring of wings, saying *zzzipp, zzzipp*. I had almost stepped on him without seeing him, so perfectly camouflaged he was, leaf-brown and motionless against the litter mosaic of the forest floor. He had startled me, and delighted me too: another surprise. What was it, I wondered. We had no names for the birds we encountered that day; the night herons and the little woodcock scarcely seemed birds at all. They were more like resident spirits, unreal manifestations of the woods, adding to its mystery and its magic.

We had come to the bend in the cinder track, and the scene changed. The dim green tunnel gave way now to a double aisle of willows, open to the sun. Their leaves were shining, and the road was filigreed with sunlight. To our right, below the road, was an open cattail marsh with a few of last year's cattails still standing, their heads tousled and bedraggled. To the left, under trees, a broad stream.

Listen! There were spring peepers in the marsh. A chorus of them down there, singing. Singing right there almost at our feet in the water at the cattail roots, and yet invisible. I wondered whether I could catch one and take it home. But I couldn't even find one. The entire assemblage was singing. First one. Then another. Then three together. Then six. Then the whole chorus. "Sing louder, peepers!" I commanded. They sang louder. "Stop, peepers!" They sang louder.

We stood and considered our next move. The stream was inviting; we would follow its course. Carl led the way, and we left the cinder road, plunging down into watery woodland. There were fallen trees here and marshy thickets; I had to dodge the snapping branches. My feet were already wet, soaked when I fell off that tree trunk. Carl wanted to wade across the stream to the island on the other side, but soon he was in above his knees, and he turned back. A turtle plooped off a stump and disappeared.

# The Lord's Woods

Beyond the next thicket we found stepping stones across the stream. If you waved your arms wildly you could hop and skip across without getting wet, pausing to wobble daringly on a loose stone in midstream. Safely across, we found ourselves on a long narrow finger of an island, with the stream to our left and the marsh on the right. A high, sandy ridge ran down the center, with a path along it, lined with birches. Ideal, I thought, for an Indian camp. I could see wigwams strung out along the path.

We each peeled a loop of birchbark and talked about the art of the Indian canoe. I had a miniature in my museum; it would have been more highly valued if it were not for the inscription, "Greetings from Sebago Lake," on its bow. It was up for trade, as a matter of fact.

We had not walked a hundred yards along the ridge before the trees thinned and then disappeared and the path plunged into the marsh. Now the path was a crooked, barely discernible file through a jungle of reeds. Carl was soon out of sight ahead of me; I could hear him crashing recklessly through the dry, brittle stalks of last year's rushes. I could no longer see ahead or in any direction: I was overwhelmed by the menacing maze that crackled like a bonfire and sent the dusty scent of broken reeds to mingle with the sulphury sweetness of the mud. If I held my stick out straight, I could prevent the reeds—some of them —from slashing my face as I stumbled blindly on, wondering how many miles and years I would be beating my way through the endless jungle, lost in this waving, green wilderness, with every leaf shooting a shining needle back at my eyes, with a shower of white sunlight through the plumes overhead, and clouds of mosquitoes rising to my arms and legs.

We burst out of the suffocating prison at last and found ourselves facing the stream again. (How far downstream we did not know.) Across the stream the marsh changed. The grass was low and level and fine, with ditches cut across it. On the left, the woods came down to the marsh like a tall, dark rampart. Far out ahead were scattered groves of trees, like islands floating in the sky, wavering and dancing above the marsh. Farther out, a punctuation mark on the air, a hawk was hovering, now soaring, now quartering low over the meadows, changing directions with a quick flip of his V-set wings.

There was a man out there!

He was out there in the middle of the marsh, and he was walking straight toward us!

Where could a man be going, crossing this wide, empty expanse of meadows? Could he see us standing here watching him? Did he live out there somewhere, a hermit perhaps, in a hut on one of those islands? An escaped convict in hiding from the law? Could that slowly moving figure, inexorably making its way towards us, all alone in this vast wilderness, could that really be man and not mirage?

Yes, it was a man indeed, progressing uncertainly, now half disappearing in a ditch, now up again on the meadow, walking with a limp, leaning on a stick. A heavy man, in overalls. And then two dark ducks flew up from a ditch in front of him and streaked off across the marsh, their quacking drifting across the meadows to us faintly.

We turned and fled from our lookout by the stream's edge, fighting our way frantically through the endless jungle of reeds, racing back along the ridge of the island, hopping across the stepping stones, and back at last to the cinder track. I wanted to run all the way back through the woods and out, but Carl discovered a stone bridge just ahead of us, where the road crossed the stream, and we ducked under it. Dim and cool there, sour smelling. My shirt was wet from running, and cold on my back. I was shivering.

On a steel beam that ran under the bridge was a bird's nest with baby birds squeaking in it. The mother bird had flown out when we rushed in, and she was sitting out on a limb over the water, making a sneezing sound. I felt like sneezing too.

We crouched under the bridge, looking down into the water and seeing the green weeds waving. The water moved them like wind in the grass. Even when there was no wind in the air, there was a wind down in the dark water, moving the strands of green weeds in the cool under the bridge. My heart was banging so loudly in my ears you could hear it a mile away, easy.

# The Lord's Woods

We waited, but nothing happened. No other sound. Perhaps the swamp man had gone away.

Here he comes!

A faint sound reached us. Tap. Shuffle. Tap. Shuffle. Coming closer. And closer. Coming down the cinder road straight towards the bridge. I couldn't breathe. My heart pounded. My shirt was icy cold. Tap. Shuffle. Tap. Now louder. Now right overhead, on the bridge. No sound now. Silence. He was still up there somewhere. I sneezed.

Suddenly there was a round red face with a big droopy mustache in the middle of it, upside down, over the rim of the bridge. "Hi, kids," it said. Not smiling, but not angry either. "Better get outa here before Mac catches you." The face disappeared. The shuffle, tap, shuffle faded down the road.

Carl raced me to the Indian Tree. Gave me a head start and beat me anyway. He always did.

# TWO

# The Explorers

FROM THAT SUMMER day of our discovery, the woods became our new-found America. To explore at first cautiously and with the disquieting sense of guilt of the intruder, but with increasing assurance as we learned our way around this secret wonderland and came to take possession of it.

It was a secret that we guarded jealously, the two of us, at least from our schoolmates. But at home the secret was revealed that very first afternoon when I tried to slip unseen through the kitchen door and was confronted by Eliza Bodkin. Her index finger arching upward imperiously, she took one look and ordered, "Out of my kitchen!" and then at half the tempo and twice the volume, *"Out—of—my—kitchen!"* So out in the vestibule I had to strip off every stitch of those mud-pied clothes, hand them in, and watch them being tossed down the stairs toward the laundry before I was permitted to race naked across the kitchen (noting with delight the makings of a Poor Man's Pudding on the table) and up the back stairs. Eliza, intoning each word as though singing a hymn and shaking her head in her beloved way, was saying for the thousandth time, "You boys will bring me with gray hairs and sorrow to the grave."

The secret lasted, in fact, until dinner. I couldn't just sit there keeping all those wonders bottled up inside me, not saying anything, could I? So the family listened patiently to the excited monologue: the Indian Tree, the water striders, the night herons, the woodcock flushed, the stepping stone island, the turtle, the swamp man, and the Phoebe's nest under the bridge. (Although I didn't know the names of all those wild things then.) Even Eliza listened, bringing in her luscious pudding, not saying a word about the knickers, already drying downstairs, cleaned and patched like new.

That night I lay awake and listened; far across the roofs of night came the high, interrupted but endless music of the marsh. Tree frogs and spring peepers and insects screaming. Out there, just beyond the football field, there just at the end of Westwood Road, a new frontier lay waiting. Dark and yet honeycombed with light, mysterious and sheltering, fascinating and still a little frightening, the frontier stretched from the white farmhouse how far we knew not, but at least to the stone bridge and beyond. Some day, perhaps Saturday morning, we would find out.

How exciting it was, that Saturday, walking out of our houses without saying where we were going, hurrying through familiar streets, giving our friends the slip, saying hello to people we knew, letting them think we were on an ordinary errand. Cutting through empty lots, stopping to pluck plantain stems and slash at each other in the beheading game, drawing out long tender stalks of grass to chew on, all the way to the *unknown!*

By the Indian Tree we paused and paid our respects, examined again the markings on the trunk, found the water striders and splashed them up a rough ride. But the tree was not our goal this day. Today we were going to walk right through these woods and out the other side. If it took all day and all night. I had half a dozen licorice ropes in my pocket. Where these woods ended and what was beyond them we must know, as desperately as Columbus had to know the limits of the ocean he sailed upon.

Down the cinder road from the Indian Tree was an open clearing with tall oaks and hickories. We passed it now, as we did before, and came upon the pipe barrier. Just beyond, we saw for the first time a grassy aisle forking to the right of the cinder road, another green tunnel roofed over by arching trees, with a

# The Explorers

footpath down its center line. Far down this green tunnel we could see bright sunlight—a clearing perhaps— with some giant trees around it.

We paused a moment at this place of decision. Carl was in favor of taking the grassy lane, and I the cinder road. Plucking up our courage, we separated. He would follow the lane, and I the road. We would keep in contact with whistles: one meant "all is well," and two signified "come quick, help." Because the two paths were almost parallel, diverging gradually, we could see each other as we walked forward. For a time at least I could see his head and shoulders moving in and out of the sunlight, now invisible behind stout tree trunks, now bobbing above the crest of a comber of cinnamon fern, with a whistle at every other step.

"It's a big pipe!" Carl shouted.

"What's a pipe?"

"What I'm walking on. The path is on top of a great big pipe that's half buried under the grass. It goes straight through the woods, I think. At least the path does. I can balance."

I could see Carl's head moving slowly, on a level now through the underbrush, suddenly to disappear with a flailing of arms, and then appear again.

"I'll come over," I shouted. He was having fun balancing.

"No. Stay on the road. And keep whistling."

So Coronado and Cortez moved forward through the trackless (almost) wilderness, haltingly, moving slowly down the legs of an ever-widening V. Now I could no longer see him through the brush, and the whistles were fainter, while my own were louder and more frequent. I was approaching the bend in the road, the two lines of willows in the sunshine and the cattail marsh now between us, the stone bridge just ahead.

At the bridge I waited, whistling, but there was no response. Have I lost him? I wondered, watching my spit swirl downstream. I waited, but Carl was nowhere to be heard, or seen. Finally, I went looking for him, running along the stream under skyscraper oaks, and there found him in a grassy clearing, with tall trees looking on, hopping back and forth where three timbers crossed the brook. A bridge of sorts: three massive, squared

27

timbers set evenly with spaces between them. Below them, at an angle, a fat black pipe crossed and the water moved westward sluggishly below it in the bed of its weed-choked channel. The three parallel timbers were at the level of the bank, and we could cross on one and return on another, or jump in midstream from one to another and then down to the pipe, or sit and dangle our legs over the water. From that day onward this place was called Three Bridges, a landmark in our woodland world, as this moment was in our lives.

From this deepest heart of the woods we looked around, Carl and I, and surveyed our secret domain. Facing us, as we sat looking south, was the grassy aisle with the pipe line that Carl had just come along; open to the sky through the cattail marsh, then dark under the tall trees all the way to that invisible point where it split from the cinder road. To the left, or eastward, was another, smaller plot of marsh bordering the stream, with billowing high woods crowding behind it like a fortress. To the right was downstream and the path that led to the stone bridge and the cinder road. We turned and looked the other way—northward—to a world we had not yet conquered. Here the grassy aisle of the pipe line continued between giant trees, although the pipe itself seemed to have disappeared underground. Far down that gauzy corridor, half hidden by trees, stood a building. Mysterious, squat, brick red, with a tall square chimney behind it. A house in a glade in the forest!

We sprawled, each on our own timber, each with a licorice rope. Here we were, alone together in a remote, harmonious, private world of our own discovering, a great blue-ceilinged, green-walled Eden filled with wonders waiting to reveal themselves, only to us. Trees towered over us, leaning together in fortuitous, but quite logical, groupings, with their distant tops glistening in the sun. Below them, the jungle of marsh and brush and weeds, silent in the early summer noon, but lively with unseen stirrings, half-heard voices of birds or squirrels or rabbits, or here and there a leaf suddenly fluttering to let us know that they were there and were watching. Over all, like a spell, the keening of the insects, the sweet greenness from the weeds on the air, and the heat from the sun-baked timber. A lazy, slowing-down-of-time feeling, when life seemed truly everlasting; there was nothing urging you on to do anything but this, and you had a vague, uneasy awareness that never, if you lived a hundred years, could any moment be better than this one, sucking on a licorice rope, lying on your back on a most accommodating timber over whispering water, looking straight up through the lace of oak leaves with the sun behind them at one small yellow bird, almost invisible, buzzing at the very top of it all, at the golden top of the world.

Listen!

There was another sound, low and distant, a throbbing *thrum, thrum, thrum, thrum,* a persistent sound so inconsequential against the other woodland noises that I was not aware of it at all—as submerged in my consciousness as my pulse beat, and like it, slow and regular. I sat up and looked around. The throbbing seemed to be coming from the dark red building far down the grassy path. Perhaps it was a factory, or a sawmill.

Without a question or discussion, we set off to investigate the intriguing sound. Walked together under giant oaks and sweet gums, up the grassy aisle toward the brick building, looming ever larger until it stood in front of us, a massive structure, Victorian-industrial in style, with enormous round-topped windows and a peaked slate roof, topped by a square, big-snouted chimney, belching sooty smoke. The throbbing of the machinery grew louder as we approached. Now it was encompassing, inescapable. *Boom, Boom,* it said. *Whoosh. Boom, boom, whoosh.* Like muffled thunder.

The front doors were open. We climbed the stone steps and looked inside.

Enormous, high, clean room with huge machinery set into the concrete, gray-painted floor. Giant iron wheels with fire-engine-red spokes, slowly revolving, half of each wheel below the floor. Massive flywheels, twice as high as a man, all polished and shining and clean. With arms on each side that moved rhythmically back and forth, seeming to drive the wheels around, like those

# The Lord's Woods

long piston rods on the steam engines of the Long Island Railroad. Up on top, little golden balls spinning around in the middle of a nest of metallic elbows. Everything joined together precisely, all balanced and interconnected in some marvelous, intricate fashion, everything moving in different and contrapuntal motions, down and around, in and out, back and forth, up and down!

It was deafening at the door of the room with the giant machinery. Clean. Hot. Smell of oil and steam. Everything burnished and shining like the engine room of a ship, like the Alexander Hamilton that we used to take to go to Sacandaga every summer, sailing up the Hudson River at night, with the searchlight sweeping the Palisades, the trees suddenly, astonishingly green in all that blackness. There were three wheels in the floor, but only two were turning; one was silent. There was no one in the room. Everything was running without anyone watching it, as if it had intelligence of its own and could be trusted.

I wondered what was happening here. What these machines, so thunderous, so firmly fixed to the concrete floor, could be making or moving. One almost expected, looking through the tall windows, to see the woods out there slowly moving past as the building sailed by. I asked Carl.

Carl said the machines were pumps. Pumping water from wells in the ground. Perhaps then—surely then—this building was the waterworks that Miss Sheard had promised to visit with us, that day we had the snowstorm!

A man came out of the door in the back and limped toward us. It was the red-faced swamp man! We stepped backward, poised for flight. He was motioning for us to come in!

Inside, the thunder was enveloping, overwhelming. Down by the timber bridge it had been a whispered heartbeat—*thrum, thrum, thrum*—but inside the big room with the wheels slowly turning and the little balls spinning and the piston arms plunging back and forth, it became a terrifying storm of sound. BOOM, BAROOM, WHOOOSH, *feeeeeeeeeee, sssssssssss*, it said, *whim, whim whim whim*. And then again BOOM, BAROOM, WHOOOSH. Everything so gleaming and polished and smooth and oily. We stood there transfixed, hypnotized by the incomprehensible motion of the machines, too complex, too ingenious to fathom, the floor vibrating, the high walls reverberating, as if a monster was caged there and tamed, but still fearsome and unpredictable. I wanted to go and run a finger along the smooth rim of one giant wheel as it rolled around, but there was a railing around each machine to keep people away.

The swamp man in his overalls was standing right over us, pointing to different parts of the machinery and shouting. It sounded like BOOM, BAROOM, triple expansion, WHOOSH flywheel, *feeeeeee* governor, *sssssssssssssssteam*, BOOM, BAROOM, WHOOSH filters, *whim whim whim whim* wells, BOOM, BAROOM millions of gallons, and while he was shouting, red-faced and serious, a silvery dragonfly came sailing through the open door and then circled around and up, soaring up to one of the high windows, lost and trapped. The swamp man led us to a wall and pointed to rows of dials as big as our schoolroom clock, some with needles that quivered and shook, and others that were scrawling jagged lines on strips of paper.

Through the door in the back of the big room we could see iron stairs descending to the lower level, where the furnaces were. Heat flowed from the stairwell in a wave, but there were men moving down in that orange inferno, their naked torsos shining, their arms and faces streaked with coal dust.

We turned to leave at last, but I turned back again and fished my last licorice rope from my pocket, handing it to our guide. He took it and shouted, "Thank you kindly," and smiled at last. I ran to join Carl, and we burst out into the sunlight.

# THREE

# The Adventurers

I OFTEN THINK of the walk through the spattered sunshine at the woods' heart that summer afternoon so many years ago. Here, not far behind the waterworks we discover a hidden pool, with steep sandy sides, and so wide that neither Carl nor I can throw a stone across it. Further on we find another grassy road with a pipe line half buried in it. On both sides now are woodland; tall, open woodland on the left of us, but on the right smaller trees, sweet gums mostly, the ground and their trunks covered and carpeted with honeysuckle. Summer silence, the deep, diminishing throbbing of the pumps. We walk on, brushing flies from damp foreheads until we find ourselves standing at the edge of a second, wider stream, at the woods' farthest margin. Across the stream a grassy bank with an apple orchard on it, a road beyond that, and still farther off, as far as one could see, endless rolling farm fields, green with the first shoots of the corn.

As we stand and watch, feeling triumphant at having reached, as last, this northernmost margin of our woods, looking out across this new and unexpected world, a horse and buggy come racing down the road, shooting up a cloud of yellow dust. A sleek red horse, a shiny black buggy with a boy in it, not much older than we are. Long after he has gone out of sight to our left, the dust hangs on the air, proving that it was real, and not a dream.

We turned back then, knowing now how far our woods extend, at least to the northward. But already we are beyond the stream and orchard in our dreams, our hearts set upon a new adventure: to see where the green fields stretch to and where the dusty road and the broad, slow-moving steam lead. Though now we have measured one dimension of our woods and found the pump house that is its beating heart, there are others to be discovered, east and west. Each horizon leads to new ones, unsuspected and even more exciting.

We stand and look long across the rippling green corn fields, hearing a killdeer cry over them; and then, with shadows lengthening as we walk, we retrace our steps. Back to the waterworks, its tall chimney now rolling out ugly folds of smoke that spread across the treetops. One more look through the door at the fascination of the big machines. Then down the grassy path to Three Bridges, along the grassy pipe-line path to the cinder road and home.

That night at dinner the family listened patiently to another account of the marvels of the woods and waterworks. My father held his water glass up to the light and admired the crystal liquid. "You know, Eddie," he said to my mother, "we don't really appreciate this water. *L'eau merveilleuse.* Clean. Sweet. Soft. Always cool, even now. Bobby, you tell your friends at the waterworks they put out a very excellent vintage." Pausing to sip, "Not exactly a Château d'Yquem 1908, but better than the miserable Moselle we had last night. *El hastisi* to it," with a wink, giving it his most awful arabic curse. Then, reflecting on that abomination of an outrage, Prohibition, and the dwindling stocks down in the cellar—whose straw-filled boxes with the dusty bottles bearing the musical French names—he grumbled that no doubt some day soon he would be glad even to have the Moselle, acid as a spinster's kiss though it was.

I thought it only natural that my woods should produce the finest water in the world.

# The Adventurers

Week by week, step by step, this secret, magical world unfolds before us. This is our dream and our sanctuary, complete and flawless, full of riches beyond our reckoning, secret and secluded from the outside world, as enchanted as if we, like Alice, had stepped through the looking glass as we entered it. In its deep heart it was as primeval and as pure as in the days of the Indian scouts, as full of mysteries and enigmatic motion as when those first white colonists ventured down these very paths, as charged with wonder and adventure as when the stealthy messengers of the rebel underground carried along its streams their intelligence to General Washington.

Sometimes we lose ourselves in its spell; sometimes we are overcome by fantasy and fever. Then we race along the woodland paths brandishing sticks, in lieu of genuine explorers' swords; we are Columbus raising his imperial banner on that first island in the Indies, we are Cortez slashing his way inland to the golden citadel, Balboa at the steaming isthmus, or Champlain moving through the silent northern forests. We are stealthy Indians, moving through the woods from shadow to shadow, never breaking a twig with our careful tread. We are Robin Hood in Sherwood Forest, battling with stout staves for the honor of Maid Marion.

"Stand back, you foul varlet," Carl snarls. "Stand back or I'll split your skull!" And Carl's stick whistles through the air.

"Stand back," I echo. "Stand back or I'll . . . (lamely) I'll knock your ears in." Our sticks whoosh through the air and crash against each other and our cries echo down the leafy aisles, and then we laugh and roll on the mossy ground, because we know the words are more from a Douglas Fairbanks movie than from history, more from the screen at Mindling's Playhouse on winter Saturday afternoons than the mouths of any knights of old. But the magic never quite leaves us. Here at the very end of Westwood Road, so close to home and school and the ordinary world, lies a trackless and unconquered continent, waiting for the bold tread of our pioneer footsteps, the dauntless courage of the explorer, waiting for *us* to claim.

We come to know the cinder road that winds through the

# The Lord's Woods

Green Cathedral (as we come to call the woods' heart), from the curve at the white farmhouse, past the big pipe barrier, through the length of the tall red maples to the feathery willows beside the marsh, then across the stone bridge, on past the waterworks to its other end at the road they call Mill Road. We know the wide grassy pipe-line path that forks to the right from the cinder road, just beyond that open corridor we call the Range. We have followed it through the woods, crossing one narrow stream on the pipe itself, crossing the marsh, crossing at Three Bridges, and then through giant trees to the waterworks.

But between the farmhouse and the woods' end are wide woodlands on both sides, and into these our steps have still been tentative. The little streams that meander through these outer regions have still to be followed to their origins. To the left and right of the cinder path and grass road are whole provinces of the unknown, unclaimed wilderness, another pond, a promontory of giant trees that runs out into the salt marsh, a majesty of oaks and maples that extend to the right of the pipe line. How far? And bordered by what still-to-be-discovered lands? Our north and south poles we now have touched, our east and west axis is not yet mapped. But we have time—a lifetime of youth is waiting ahead, not hurrying us, not lingering, but moving at its natural, easy pace. We will know it all, Carl and I. We will explore and conquer this America of ours, we will make this our private paradise. To know it and, by knowing, own it, and then go forth beyond our woodland bounds, answering the urgent beckonings of field and farm and road and stream, the distant marsh horizon, the island of trees floating out there seemingly detached from the earth in the shimmering heat of summer, and the row of trees beyond the last ones we can see.

We have no words for it, Carl and I, but in our hearts we know that it is beautiful, and everlasting, and precious. This is the first of our discoveries.

# FOUR

# Awakening

*The little rabbit explodes from the clump of dried ferns at our feet and scampers down the path ahead of us, its white puff of a tail bouncing. I try to get my bow into position but the arrows scatter on the ground and before anything can be retrieved, inserted, drawn, or loosed the cottontail has disappeared. Today is my eleventh birthday, and I got this really peachy bow-and-arrow set this morning. It's the first one I've ever had, except for that baby stuff with rubber cups on the arrows. These are real target arrows with red and white silk around the shafts. You have to pull with all your strength to get the arrow back all the way, so that the tip is near the string. I shot one this morning in the garden and it sailed right over the garage and into Old Lady Richardson's, and of course she yelled at me when I went to get it. I thought she was going to run out and grab it, but she just stood in the door and yelled.*

*She doesn't like me and my brother Rich to go through the hole in the hedge. We do it every day on the way to school. She never gets tired yelling.*

"I wasn't ready for that cottontail. You hold the other arrows and I'll put this one on the string and hold it like this. Maybe we can sneak up on that cottontail again. You can have the next shot.

"I think he scooted off there through that thicket. You go around the other side of it and maybe you'll scare him out my side. Boy, Carl, that's a really tangled up mess, isn't it? Everything's got thorns on it. Shhhh. I thought I saw something moving under there. There he goes! Heck, that was only a little gray bird. Owww! I'm caught. Wait a minute, till I get free. Heck, I caught my knickers and tore them. Just a little hole though.

"There he goes! Hey! Hey! There he goes!"

*I missed. It's not so easy, really. They run awfully fast and zigzag too. I didn't miss by much, but my arm was shaking a little.*

"Boy, there's one arrow that's good-by forever. Right into the middle of that brier patch.

"Here, you take the bow and I'll carry the arrows. Only, if you get a shot don't shoot into a brier patch. 'Cause I don't want to lose any more arrows. I only have five left.

"We can go through the woods on the right of the pipe line. I've seen rabbits up in there."

*The woods are so different this time of year. They're even quieter now in the middle of March than in summer. No peepers calling, no humming insects, and hardly a bird around. You can hear some outside sounds, even when you're deep in the middle of the woods. Dogs barking somewhere, and the* thump, thump, thump *of the waterworks. But mostly you don't hear anything but the* creak-creak *of a tree branch in the wind. Sometimes the trees creak at each other, as if they were talking. It's really still winter on my birthday. St. Patrick's Day, you know. I always get a cake with green candles and pistash ice cream. My father wears a green tie. But this year the snow's all melted and it's not too cold in the sun.*

*It's like a different world here in the woods this time of year. Not a green closed-in world like in summer, not a brown-and-gold world like in fall, but a kind of black-and-gray world. Gray trees with black branches, gray ground covered with dead leaves, pools of black water around the tree roots, rusty black pipe line.*

# Awakening

*You can really see where everything is—where every tree stands, where all the pipes go, and all the logs and sticks lying around. You can see much farther through the woods, too, but you really can't see anything but a kind of gray-pink cloud of trees, all merging together in the distance. Everything crackles when you walk, because the wind has scattered twigs all over the paths.*

"Let's walk like Indians without stepping on twigs, okay? See who can be the quietest. I won't talk any more, either.

"Crows. That's what they were. Four big black crows. You couldn't hit one in a million years with an arrow. Not flying anyway. And they always see us first.

"Now you've lost another arrow! I told you you couldn't hit a crow! Ah, heck!"

*Not a sound anywhere now. Just the two of us, in the middle of the forest, with trees leaning in all around us. Nothing in the trees. Nothing in the sky, nothing on the ground under the trees. Quiet, as if waiting for something to happen. Holding its breath, waiting for spring to come, for animals to awaken, for birds to fly in and sing, for leaves to unfold and everything to come to life. It's like the very beginning of the year, which should be now in March, this windy day in March, not in frozen January.*

*It's not true that nothing is happening. Under the trees are these funny little greenish-brown humpy things. Do you know what they are? Skunk cabbage coming up! Pick one and smell it if you don't believe me. I found that out last year. It smells terrible, just like a skunk, like the one that got under our cottage one time at Sacandaga.*

*You can tell that it will be spring soon because the buds on all the trees and bushes are bigger. Bite one and it's all green inside. Tiny leaves all folded up and crinkled, getting ready to pop open when the sun warms them. The mosses under the trees are getting greener too. And the brier thickets look like green mist from a distance. The year is beginning now, and you can hardly wait to see it change from day to day.*

"Look, a butterfly! So early. A big dark-brown butterfly with yellow edges to his wings, fluttering along close to the ground. I know that one, it's in my Butterfly Guide. It's called Mourning

39

# The Lord's Woods

Cloak. I wonder what that means? Mourning. Look—a squirrel!"

Through the webbed vault of the forest he came, flying light as a shadow on his dancer's feet, now racing down a slendering branchlet to its bending tip, now soaring across a gaping well of air, now sitting silent to survey his next feat of derring-do. A gray plummet, a bushy-tailed pendulum, a daredevil aerialist on his treetop trapeze. So sure of foot, so swift and balanced on his swaying swing, is it bravery or mere bravado? Now quick and reckless, now still and safe in the hollow of a trunk, flicking his long tail like a signal flag, twittering scorn and challenge to the watchers just discovered far below. Caught here in the middle of some errand of private urgency, or no urgency, or perhaps just the first springtime ecstasy. And we shot him!

A gray squirrel alone and alive, so bright of eye, so delicately put together, so much at home and free in his airy realm of gray limbs, gray leaves, gray sky. Now head down on tree trunk, peering at a crazy upside-down world with ground for sky, now spying from a tiny crotch, now skipping lightly like an acrobat on a canvas trampoline. A clown or jester perhaps, or more an elfin gladiator, knowing death to be all around him everywhere in his treetop circus, beside him at every leap, from fall, or hawk, or hunter. Still leaping this way and that to avoid, for this split second only the eventual, and final, encounter. Alert and shy, graceful and afraid, knowing in his bones and sinews distances and heights that could be dared, knowing spring and recovery, climb and retreat. Understanding the security of silence and immobility, or if not understanding, knowing. A small, very much alive gray squirrel, at home in his woods (not ours), on a quiet March morning, wishing us no ill, doing us no harm, and we shot him.

Did you pull the bow, or did I? I cannot believe that I did it, but if I was the one, my guilt has blotted out the moment of fateful action.

It was our last arrow, that I know. When we saw the little sky creature, he was high in a red maple, a small, still silhouette. When we crept nearer, he moved reluctantly, by starts and sudden stops, across the bending branches, and we followed. His

# Awakening

undulating leaps and our pursuit took him at last to the very edge
of his world, the open corridor we called the Range, and there
he paused, facing a barrier of empty air. We moved nearer while
he sat and watched and scolded fifty feet above our heads. The
arrow fitted, the trembling bow drawn full, the arrow loosed, a
puff of fur, a clutching and then a slow release of stiffened legs,
a pinwheel (how awkward, how disorganized) through the tree.
And lay at last, broken and bleeding, the eyes gone blind, the
legs awry, at our feet.

Our cries of victory, our pride at this wholly unexpected feat
of archery had deserted us halfway down the sickening fall and
now we were numb and stricken, appalled at this evil, irremedi-
able thing we had done. So quick to die, so little space, so thin a
line between the living, breathing, life-enjoying creature and the
sad, dead heap! Standing here over it, ashamed of ourselves and
choking with remorse, wishing the arrow could have somehow
been diverted in flight (who would have dreamed we could
actually hit a squirrel so high in a tree!), the little animal re-
established on his perch to go his way on whatever sally of private
importance or of simple joy had crossed his fate with ours.

We buried him beside the last tree on the edge of the Range,
and I broke the arrow and tossed away the bow. We walked home
silently, thinking of squirrel in tree and bird in brush and knowing that from that day onward they would be forever safe from
our mischief.

Walked home filled with guilt and grieving, harried to the very
edge of the woods by a gang of outraged, angry jays, heaping
scorn on our unhappy heads.

# FIVE

# Stirring

SPRING IS COMING: life is return-
ing to the woods. It is visible in some new sign every day. Not
always in the slow, subtle changes of form and color that are
continuous and that often scarcely enter our awareness, but in
swift surprises and sudden advances that were not here yesterday.
The days are cold and wind-whipped between the sun-warmed
ones, and even on days of sun the skies are patched with puffy
white clouds sailing, so that one may be walking in mild springtime one moment and chill winter shadow the next. There is
still frost on the greening blades of grass each morning, and we
get one late wet snow. But even with this setback there is no
denying this shy, reluctant spring: each day the woods seem not
quite so bleak, so bare, so empty as the day before.

Each warm day we see a sign to excite us and whet our anticipation. Now a day when nebulae of tiny gnats revolve above the
melting snow pools, now a day when gangs of crows come alive
with bawdy raillery and much chasing over the tree tops. Now
a day when the sweet soliloquy of our first bluebirds—the very
first bluebirds of our lives—drifts through the gray-green haze
of branches, and we find them, those incredible blue presences,
four of them, making leisurely forays around the Range.

The calendar now says April, and though the blade of the wind

43

may still have a cutting edge, and the branches still creak and complain, the winter is almost over. One day you look down the Grassy Road of the pipe line and it is green, and the web of trees no longer looks gray or gray-green, but is tinged with palest pink. All overnight the buds of the red maples have swelled, soon to break. Along the bend in the Cinder Road, the willows now are golden-green although still no leaf has shown: it is the green of April bud and twig and branch. Along the paths the browns and drabs of snow-packed leaves show here and there a parting where a clump of pale fiddleheads are pushing up, or the green leaves of skunk cabbage, or even an outcropping of violets. It has been this way for a thousand years or more, we know, but somehow this spring is our spring, a pageant of discoveries and delights.

The stream beside the Indian Tree is swollen with the vanished snows and days of rain, and in the lowest places it has overbrimmed its banks and spread black pools among the maples. We make our way slowly, skirting this tree, hugging the trunk with one arm as we wheel around it, threading that tangle, leaping from clump of grass to knob of roots, clutching at any helping hand of branch or vine. Like two uncertain frogs we slither and hop our way through these woodlands to the west of the Cinder Road, keeping now to the stream bank, now skirting in wide detours; our boots caked black, tears in our jackets appearing here and there where sleeves and brier join in temporary combat.

This is new territory for us; we seem to be taking a curving course westward through the bogged red maples, for the stream is a crooked one. Its water shines now blue, now cloud gray in the changing light of early afternoon, and leaves are moving in it. We pause on a high place beside a giant tree whose trunk soars straight up with no branches for a hundred feet or more, surely the monarch of this part of the woods. Somewhere in the distance a bird is calling, a shivery sneezy call we've heard before; yes, it's the little gray bird that nests under the Stone Bridge—the Phoebe. And there's another, farther off on the left, that seems to answer it.

We moved forward again, and the woods grow thin, and underfoot are tumbled tussocks of high grass, with scattered smaller trees growing among them. Suddenly we can see the wide marshland directly ahead of us, flooded in places, still gray and wintry with no sign of spring. We walk through and over the tussock grass until the water reaches our boottops with each step; then, each of us perch atop a tussock and, clinging to a slender tree stem, we survey the marsh. To our right runs the line of woods we had looked back on from Stepping Stone Island, and there we can see the tongue of marsh and the wide stream between the woods and the island. Ahead of us, the flat, ditch-laced marshland stretching far to westward, with its islands of trees now gaunt and leafless. Dotted here and there across the marsh is the flotsam of winter storms: weather-whitened driftwood, fragments of wooden boxes, windrows of salt hay. Some day when it is no longer flooded we will walk across this marsh, leaping the ditches like the Swamp Man, all the way to the islands and beyond.

Our stream turns left again, and we return to it, following it along the edge of the tussocky grassland. Here it doubles back, and we find a farmer's field across the stream, not yet plowed, the dead and crumpled cornstalks scattered by wind and rain, and on our side of the stream, a file of willows. And between the farm field and the willows, our stream flows into a tiny pond! A secret pond we had never suspected, hidden here with reeds around it, dark and deep, but a blue mirror to the sky. We move around it slowly, under the willows, and discover that the stream runs out the other side of the pond in a wide, straight ditch into the marsh. Where the ditch begins we climb a willow tree for another survey.

With the added height we can see farther across the marsh, with its crisscrossing ditches, its distant islands; we can even see the course of the big stream that curves through the marsh along Stepping Stone Island; it makes an S-turn at a wide place, joins another even wider stream and flows on westward, no longer visible. Where?

Off to the left another surprise, but not as exciting as our expanding marsh because it is no longer wilderness, but a golf course. It is sodden from the spring floods, its fairways half submerged, its flat, untended acres stretch right up to, and even into, the marshland. Here and there little groves and scattered single cedar trees, shaped like dark plumes, interrupt the flat landscape; in years to come we will find owls in those cedars. Hidden from our view are little pockets of true fresh-water bogs, filled with sphagnums, where we will, in the next year or two, find orchids: Arethusa, Calopogon, and Pogonia. On the fairways themselves, in winters to come, the larks and buntings from the north, in their wind-blown flocks, will sweep down on the stubble to feed.

But look! Far off across the farthest edge of the golf course, beyond the broken reeds at the edge of the marsh, beyond the broad, flooded marshland, even beyond that distant, tiny picket fence that we would some day find to be an abandoned railway trestle and walk its entire length, out there floating on the distant horizon, so dimly seen, so ephemeral as to be something half-imagined and half real, against a strand of lavender sky—could it be? the silhouettes of towers? A jagged, slotted, shadow low against the sky, with half a dozen taller spires—yes, that must be man-made, must be the skyscrapers of the city! How far away it was across that endless meadow. How silent and remote, a citadel like King Arthur's Camelot, but sunken low against the earth, with only the topmost battlements standing there, luminous in the lowering afternoon sunshine. How long we looked and dreamed across this bowl of sky and earth and mystery I cannot remember now, but it was long enough to imprint every shadow and contour of the city on my memory until this day. To fix for us forever our whereabouts in space, our position on earth relative to the giant city we had visited, by train and even in my father's Franklin, but had never seen this way, across the endless earth.

We come down to earth again and circle the little pond to find a crossing and suddenly see, to our astonishment, an enormous turtle surface in the dark waters. A giant, vicious head, long neck, and a rough, black shell a full two feet along the back. The neck cranes, the beady, prehistoric eyes survey the sky for a moment, and then as we rush forward to see this monster closer and perhaps, somehow, catch it, it sinks beneath the surface

# Stirring

without a ripple, disappearing like a hallucination and leaving us to ask each other if we had truly seen and not imagined this thing. Though we search for another hour and beat the water with sticks, throw stones and raise a mighty hullabaloo, we never catch another glimpse of it, and in all the years that we visit that little pond, in every season, that ancient giant of a snapping turtle remains a mystery, and lost forever.

No wide and wondrous vistas graced the southern margins of our woods, no far horizons with their floating islands in the sky, no purple shadows of towers pale and shining against the lavender of evening sky. No farms and fields to call us farther on, no beckening of endless marsh and meadow. Here was the raggle-taggle littoral of man's domain, the frontier between the world of wild unknown and of known and everyday. Here a grid of parallel streets ran down to a dead-end at the woods. Nearer to the village the houses huddled together in seeming congeniality, but farther down toward the wilderness the vacant lots increased, the houses grew meaner and smaller, until at the farthest end of some streets there were no houses anywhere, just broken sidewalks and cratered streets with grass growing everywhere, reclaiming for their own the site of some sad, forgotten dream of some long-skedaddled developer. At the far end of every street, the high, forbidding (but to us inviting) wall of the high woods.

Some of these streets were more interesting (exciting and a little challenging, too) than others, for it was to their neglected and weedy ends that the poorest and most prolific families of the town had come. Here, where the streets had all but disappeared and no traces of sidewalks could be found, were amazing little patchwork houses all askew, fascinatingly cluttered, storm-stained, open-doored, sagging, their windows busted and replaced with paper, yards where no flowers, or even weeds, would grow, but which blossomed with an abundant harvest of rusting automobile parts, lumber, broken furniture, pipes, and plumbing appliances; here a mammoth once-red upholstered chair with its guts hanging out obscenely, naked to wind and weather; here a bedspring with a bonnet of live hens; here a landlocked, bottomless rowboat filled with bricks; and here a stranded bathtub. Always, around these houses, winter or summer, late or early, a gaggle of thin-faced, snot-nosed, towheaded children of all ages, dressed like scarecrows, always dirty, almost always hostile. How marvelous their freedom, their undisciplined life (even the smallest one smokes!), how near they are to our woods, and how rarely they ever enter it!

We came this way infrequently and with some trepidation, for we had heard it said that all of them—even the girls—were wild, unprovoked fighters and the mothers foul-tongued harri-dans of imposing girth who could curl your ears at three hundred yards. We heard it whispered too among our elders, but never proved, that most of the bicycles, mailboxes, fence posts, and other disappearing movables around the village could be traced eventually to these close-guarded, darksome precincts.

Behind the houses, at the ends of the streets, where the woods and the vacant lots came together, there was a no man's land, a border zone of brier tangles, interpersed irregularly with pot-holes filled with water and bulrushes. Here our woods began, the same woods we could enter from Westwood along the Cinder Road. Here you could walk down any street and disappear into the forest.

The woods were wide here and grew wider the farther east-ward you went from the white farmhouse, for the Cinder Road angled northeastward from its entrance, and the southern margin made an ever-widening angle with both the Cinder Road and the nearer Grassy Road. No trails, or very few, wandered through these unspoiled, primeval trees. They were the tallest we had found: tulips, oak, hickory, ash, and maple, soaring, dark, and empty. Two minor streams bisected this area, both flowing west-ward across the wood, one continuing down to (and past) the Indian Tree to the snapping turtle pond and then into the marsh, the other into the cattail marsh between the Grassy Road and the willows, at Stepping Stone Island; both these streams afforded our easiest routes of access.

At the extreme eastern corner of our woods (we would come soon to call this section the Big Woods) a road, Mill Road by name, ran north through fields. It crossed one wide creek, and at this same spot a single, grass-grown railroad track crossed the road, and plunged into the woods. Here it ran parallel to the road, through a magnificent grove of oaks, and then swung sharply left, and on into the waterworks. This was the way the coal cars came in to feed the furnaces for the pumps.

We made these little-used (once or twice each year?), rusty tracks and the grass-grown, half-buried ties between them our thoroughfare.

The creek here—it was the upper end of the one we had watched flowing under the Tree Bridges, under the Stone Bridge, around Stepping Stone Island, and out into the marsh—wound into the heart of our sanctuary, and where it entered the woods there was a thick tangle, grown up in bracken and blackberry in summer, a fine place to hide our bicycles before we entered the hushed magic of the woods. From this hideaway a wide, dry path followed the creek along its banks, with only a few fallen trees to scramble over.

These were the southern and eastern limits of our forest playground, best known and least stimulating of all our margins, because they were in reality our near shore. Sometimes we entered the woods at the ends of the mean streets and plunged across the Big Woods. Sometimes, entering along the Cinder Road, we walked up the pipe-line path and turned right at random, to explore. And always ended, no matter how we turned and dallied and meandered, within sight of a littered yard, a flapping of laundry, a rutted street, a vacant overgrown lot, and within range of discordant sounds of squalling children, shrieking women, and barking mongrels. So we avoided this frontier when we could (it made a welcome short cut in a storm), even though the Big Woods that swept up to it were wild and beautiful and untouched and concealed within their depths two perfect, immaculately designed glades, like two stages awaiting some medieval idyl to unfold.

# SIX

# The Unfolding

THE SPRING WARMS and the woods green slowly day by day, bringing each time we visit a faint intensification of the single hue, that pale, golden, washed-in-the-sun, fragrant green. First the merest half-imagined shadow of it, then the barest tinge, and then the most subtle reality, a wash in water color, a verdant film that strengthens, deepens, fills, and grows as if each night a painter with the most delicate of touch is adding tiny brush strokes from the same monochromatic palette. Slowly at first, imperceptibly, but then in sunny days with daring splashes of color, the woods turn green. Along the Cinder Road, and in the swampy woods on either side, before the green had been the rose; clouds of buds from the red maples had burst open, sheathing the sky in pink lace, then in a single night carpeting the Cinder Road all softly red, like drifts of rose-red snow.

Now all is coming green; the willows by the cattail marsh are first to leaf out, and then the spicebush and alders down along the streams, mixed in with clumps of pearly-tipped pussy willow. In every wet place bright emerald carpeting appears, of grasses and ground cover, of ferns and skunk cabbage, violets and ground ivy, and of mosses, each springing to life in its proper place in the ordained, traditional procession, and each a miracle.

# The Lord's Woods

We know the bounds of our woods now, on every side, from the white farmhouse at one end to the far creek and the farm fields beyond, from the golf course and marshlands on the west to the Mill Road at the eastern boundary. We know its landmarks, too, its streams, its Cinder Road, its grassy pipe lines through the woods, each pipe line strung along its length with little chapels in the forest, where strange wheels and pipe connections seem to mark the location of the wells. We are familiar with the workings of the pump house and some of the men who work there— even those grimy galley slaves who stoke the furnaces by hand in the hottest summer weather. We've watched the coal cars riding up on the trestle and spewing out their dusty fuel, we've walked all around the concrete rim of the settling pools and played games among the stacks of pipe stored on the Pipe Farm. We've balanced our way along the railway track; splashed our way across the Stepping Stones and out into the rushy jungle, walked the Range, and inspected the wooden barrier at its northern end, finding splinters of bullets in the sand below it, where the policemen's targets were sometimes pinned. We've run down trails and pulled ourselves up trees and fallen into almost every muddy hole there is. We know the look of the woods in summer, autumn, winter, and now in onrushing spring.

But these woods are still a mystery, for we do not yet know who lives here, beyond the rabbits, the turtles along the streams, a few vague, half-familiar birds, and the mice whose miniature paths we can see winding through the grass. Who can say that these woods they call the Lord's Woods are truly ours until we come to know and make friends with all the inhabitants of these acres: those who live here and those others who come, as we do, to visit.

This spring it is the wildflowers that we seek out first. Carl has a new wildflower book, and we will not only learn the names of those that grow in our woods, but bring some of them home alive. In the beginning I am somewhat dubious, but Carl's enthusiasm is infectious. We will convert a tiny patch of his garden, that cool and shady corner along our fence, into a miniature

# The Unfolding

woodland. We'll make special collecting expeditions to the woods, to discover, identify, and bring back wildflowers, planting them around a half-hidden pool (a sunken birdbath) we will construct under his flowering dogwood. My father even gives me permission to add some wild plants (no weeds!) to his "rock garden," that mound of earth and rocks with its curving slate steps on our side of the fence. Each of us will have in a small space a mirror of our woods, with the flowers blooming here to announce in every season their blooming in the wild.

Now our explorations have a secret purpose: we take small tools and paper bags with us and carry knapsacks. These are quick forays, for we must minimize the time between digging and replanting; bicycles are required, at least to the wood's edge and back. Now we roam the trails with eyes on the ground. Here a constellation of Red Trillium, further on Jack-in-the-Pulpit, and we each take two; there a blanket of wild Lily of the Valley, a clump of violets, then a dash home. Another time it is a carpeting of Spring Beauty and one treasured Hepatica, cautiously removed to guard the roots.

Other days we go in search of ferns. How many different kinds there seem to be, even in that one stretch of woods beyond Three Bridges! Cinnamon Fern clumps, so hard to dig, so tenacious of root. If we cut them through will they live or die? Is that corner of Carl's garden dark and damp enough for them, even if he waters every day? We look through his book and find that we've collected New York Fern, and Bracken, Sensitive Fern, and Hay-scented, with its tender fragile fronds that give forth an aroma when rubbed between the palms of mowed grass, or perhaps even more like some of the spices in Eliza's kitchen. Christmas Fern too comes home with us, and then one day we come upon the one we never even hoped for, that rarest treasure of them all, that beauty of the deep woods, the Maidenhair Fern. This is the gem, with its delicate leaves strung like beads along a necklace curving inward (so feminine, and yet why the name?); this is a glory to be guarded. Not to be transplanted now, but to be kept secret, hoped for, watched over, to be half-hidden by a brushy barricade of our own making—watched and waited for until that day when there are so many that one for Carl's garden will not be missed.

Here are other prizes to be gathered, two or three at a time, to be rushed home, carefully planted, watered, and watched each day for signs of success—or failure. False Solomon's-Seal and that much rarer true Solomon's-Seal, with its hanging carillon of bells. Bloodroot and Wild Geranium, Wood Anemone and Ground Ivy.

Then one day beside the Deep Ditch, sheltered in a grove of young red oaks, an almost unbelievable find—a thriving, flourishing bed of Trailing Arbutus. We take one tendril and leave the rest; it goes into the ground beneath Carl's stripling oak, complete with leaves and mulch from the original site. It thrives for a few weeks, then seems to cease its growth and linger unchanged through the summer without a new leaf, and then it dies. Perhaps the most exciting find of all—how could we have missed for so long such a sweeping panoply—Pink Lady's Slipper! Carl took half a dozen and I took, with misgivings, two, and still we left two hundred or more strewn across that grove of oaks between Cinder Road and grassy pipe line north of the wide stream. Mine died quickly (too much sun?) but his survived and bloomed each year precisely on the day that woodland host spread its pink cloud across the leaf-strewn ground, to signal for us that the time had come to go back and see them, glowing from within like Japanese lanterns, and be glad.

This was the spring of the Pussy Willow and the Sassafras, and of acorns planted, never to be seen again. I even brought home and carefully nurtured one small shoot of Poison Ivy, but that cannot compare to the day Carl tried to transport four tremendous, fetid, stinking Skunk Cabbages under his sweater, both of us pedaling furiously in a futile effort to create our own breeze and blow away the noxious fumes. Does he still remember burying his shirt and sweater behind the garage? Alas, the torn and crumpled Skunk Cabbage wilted and died without ever putting up a fight. It needs wet feet, we found.

# The Unfolding

Something else we found that spring—the birds! We never went searching for them, and we rarely even looked closely at the ones we encountered. But as the spring grew warmer and the woods greener, we slowly became aware that everywhere we went we were surrounded by birds. Small dark birds in thickets and tangles, bright little nervous birds in the understory of the forest, elusive camouflaged birds in copses and clearings. Big ungainly birds in the treetops, in the marsh, and along the streams, so many different shapes and sizes and colors! In the early mornings of our Saturday expeditions the woods echoed with a confusion of voices; a chorus of whistles and chirps and warblings and chattering. Only a few were known to us, names left over from our fifth-grade nature walks with Miss Wing: we recognized the Red-winged Blackbirds, the Robins, flickers, bluebirds, and meadowlarks in the fields. There was a chart with many birds brightly colored, all crowded together in the most impossible juxtapositions, that hung on our schoolroom wall. In the school library were pamphlets, each with colored pictures of a single bird, put out by the Audubon Society. We had looked at all of them. Perhaps as many as twenty different birds are now familiar to us, but this spring the woods are teeming with fascinating strangers.

One day Carl bought, and the next day I got one, too, a little pocket guide to the birds. It fit right into our pockets, and there was a picture in color on each page, with a story telling where that bird is found and how to distinguish it from the others. I took it to bed and pored over it late into the night, caught in thrall by the endless variety of them all, the marvelous names, the curious calls and songs, and what was meant by "shy denizen of the deepest woods." From that day onward one or both of us brought our Reed Guides with us on our explorations and tried to guess, when we saw or heard a bird, what its proper name might be. But in that spring of our novitiate we had no idea, no true awareness of the vast concourse that poured through the Lord's Woods in May and lost us in their numbers and variety. We knew they were all around us; the woods on all sides rang with their wild, insistent music. But whether this one was a Cerulean Warbler, or that one an Olive-backed Thrush, we never could be certain.

A few, to be sure, were easy. The first startling, almost unbelievable shock of scarlet moving through the treetops could only be—page 117—a Scarlet Tanager! The little inquisitive bird with the black mask and yellow belly, flirting in and out of the roadside blackberry patch—that was a Maryland Yellowthroat. We decided, after some debate and certain misgivings, that we'd seen and heard some Wood Thrushes, Towhees, and a Kentucky Warbler (our first of many bad mistakes). But this was our plant-finding spring, not a spring for birds, and most of the winged things that flew in and out of the shadows and sang unseen were background, incidental furnishings.

Then one day, something happened that swung us around and broadened our outlook, giving us a new orientation and an even more exciting pursuit. Walking up the Cinder Road one day in early summer, we came upon a band of boys, acquaintances of ours, from our own school. One or two were older than we were, one was younger. Two of the boys had binoculars hanging from their necks, and they were slowly coming up the Cinder Road toward us, *looking at birds!* We, who thought we owned these woods and were the only ones to search out the plants and animals and were getting to know the birds, were now confronted by a band of interlopers. We stopped and said our cautious hellos, and they asked us what we had seen, without a trace of astonishment or embarrassment that we were all engaged in this most unboyish of activities.

"Rue Anemone, we found," I ventured.

"And a White Hellebore blooming," added Carl.

"Birds, we mean, not flowers! Aren't you looking for birds? You've got a Reed Guide in your pocket."

"Oh," we answered, mixing pride and diffidence. "Towhee and Catbird and Maryland Yellowthroat (our new discovery!) and Wood Thrush and . . ."

"And Scarlet Tanager and Crow and Redstart," Carl added, and then we ran out of names.

# The Unfolding

"How about you?" we asked. To listen, embarrassed and a little jealous, as they rattled off the names of the birds they have seen already in just the entrance to the woods and around the Range. A dozen warblers and other birds we had seen in our books and nowhere else—there in our woods that very day!

"Didn't you even get an Ovenbird?" the oldest one asked in disbelief. We shook our heads.

"Well, just listen! They're singing in the woods all around you!" We listened, hearing only the symphonic chorus on all sides.

"There!" the whole group shouted. "That *wee-cher, weee-cher, weee-cher!*"

"Oh, that," we answered, lamely. "Couldn't find out what that was."

"Well, that's an Ovenbird," he said. "Commonest bird on this side of the woods. Walks along the ground. You fellas sure don't know anything about birds."

"We know where there's some Trailing Arbutus."

"Yeah, so do we," said the youngest one. "And don't you touch it. It's against the law!"

# SEVEN

# Expanding

THE NEXT AUTUMN, I made friends with the group.

Carl and I were still close friends, but we were beginning to move imperceptibly along diverging paths. We still went to the woods together, roaming, exploring, occasionally collecting wild plants to be brought home to his woods garden. (I had given up on my rock garden; it was just too sunny and too dry.) Often I would whistle our call (a passable imitation of an oriole) from my window or the garden, and he would come to his window or the fence and we would talk flowers or animals or birds. But now, more and more his plans would include friends of his own age and from his own school, or girls. Often I would go to the woods alone, or with other schoolmates. Sometimes I would meet friends by chance in the woods and join them in whatever sense or nonsense occured to us, for no longer were the woods a secret place known to a jealous few; they had now become a well-known playground wilderness. Often I would meet members of the group and tag along. My passion, ever since that eye-opening meeting on the Cinder Road, increasingly was birds.

The boys we met that day who had shamed us with the Oven-bird were all members of a close-knit little coterie which called itself the Bird Club. The club was, in fact, an unofficial extra-curricular activity whose guiding spirit and adviser was the

59

school's science teacher, although the group included boys from the neighborhood who were enrolled at other schools. At the time we first encountered them in the woods, there were eight members in the club, ranging in age from ten to fifteen.

We never met them all at once, but singly or in small groups. We would come upon them along the Cinder Road, or the Grassy Road, or in the Range, or suddenly around the bend of a trail through the Big Woods. One day perhaps it would be the brothers Bob and Benny, the next time Roy and Duke, again it might be Bob and Bud and Finny, or Roy and Howie. Often, with them, the slim, slight terrifyingly authoritarian figure of the science teacher, Mr. Harrower. Actually, the boys of the Bird Club were no strangers to us. We had known them all since kindergarten days, had played with them on school teams, had fought with them in street fights, had sat around birthday party tables with them; Roy's father was our family physician and Duke was in my class, but none of them were among my closest boyhood companions.

Now, seeing them so often in the woods, searching the same thickets and scanning the same horizons, we felt a kindred spirit. Gradually, as my knowlege increased, I found myself accepted and included in the group; the birds I discovered were sought out with interest, the birds they found were pointed out to me.

They all had binoculars and so I had to have some, too. First I borrowed, and then begged, and finally had bestowed upon me for a birthday present, my father's racetrack pair. The fantastic first day of the binoculars, running all the way to the woods, putting the glasses up a dozen times to fence posts, telephone poles, rooftops, clouds, finally sighting and finding in the lens a little woodpecker! Now suddenly all the birds closed in, came down from the treetops and in from the marsh and looked me in the eye! Now I could detect, even from a distance, all those telltale marks that distinguish one bird from others like it: faint lines over the eye, pale wing stripes, a wash of olive on the breast, the curve of bill or cut of tail. And now, more often included in the walks of the group, with Mr. Harrower by my side to instruct, chide, correct, and counsel, my knowledge leaped ahead. Now the Reed Pocket Guide was no longer adequate: I needed more comprehensive, better-illustrated manuals, and so saved my allowance—25 cents each Friday—to buy them.

That was the autumn that I first walked Rowdy to the woods, a red-coated, long-trousered cocker spaniel. Rowdy was the family pet but I was his master; he slept at the foot of my bed and followed me from room to room all day, conversed with me in little mewing sounds, and in his subtle way, ruled the household. The softest upholstered chair in the house was his favorite snoozing spot; he would lie with his nose drooping over one arm one eye half-cocked for Eliza, who might come at any moment and send him off with a cry of "Look at that Rowdy—sitting up there like he was a governor!"

Rowdy loved the woods. All the way to the entrance he would run in frantic circles, nose to ground, tracking now a squirrel, now a rabbit, now an oppossum or a raccoon; keeping me always in sight but weaving his own wild drunken way across the woods with eyes alight and tongue lolling. He ran a hundred feet for every foot I walked; came to ditches and sailed across them with ears out like wings, dashed into thickets, and came to dead stops crying for me to come and extricate him. But always at the watery ditch at the edge of the cattail marsh disaster waited: a run, a soaring leap, a splash, a scramble soaking wet up the opposite bank. Rowdy knew enough about momentum to knock open our swinging pantry door; if his first run at it failed he would invariably start again with a longer run and hurl himself against it, with success. But that one ditch forever fooled him, or did it? I sometimes thought he liked the sheer drama of it: the instant transition from sleek, silky, beautifully groomed spaniel into sopping, mud-caked, bedraggled mutt. It was his reminder to me that he was still a free spirit, and no mere house dog.

On the way home the tables were turned. The distance he had run in circles, the brooks leaped or missed, now exacted their penalty, and a lagging, dragging, reluctant Rowdy would have to be urged on, waited for, and told, as he turned in hopefully (knowing full well where he lived) at each front path . . . first the Walters, then the Hewletts, then the Goodmans, "Come on Rowdy, we're not home yet." And Rowdy giving me that plaintive look that only cockers know, saying clearly, "I know it, but damn it, I'm pooped."

Now it was no longer true that were we were the only ones who made these woods our playground. Increasingly, it seemed to us, the boys (and much more rarely the girls) of our village found their way into these magic precincts to roam and play and learn their secrets. In those years, before more formidable barriers were erected at either end of the Cinder Road, riders on horseback would come through. Sometimes, when you were standing silently on the Grass Road or the Cinder Road, you would be aware suddenly that right behind you were a horse and rider, or even three or four. We didn't mind the riders. They were quiet, and they disturbed the woods but little; in fact, they seemed to belong.

What we did mind was the boy scouts. Often on Saturday mornings the entire woods seemed to echo with their shouts and whistles. Some of their scoutmasters and patrol leaders used police whistles but the younger ones seemed to communicate with hoots and howls and screams. We cursed their aimless chasing and their ceaseless noise; we wondered what kind of Indian scouts they thought they were: stealth was what we supposed they should be practicing. Over in one corner of the open woods west of the pump house they had a camp, a circular clearing where they pitched their tents and lit their fires, and from which they sallied forth to butcher all the saplings for a hundred yards around. We wondered why no one ever taught them how to use an ax or fell a tree: their little popinjay hatchets seemed to fray trees down, not chop them. Leaving always a three- or four-foot stump, or often the sapling toppled, still attached, left there broken and disgraceful. The trees around the clearing were not the only ones subject to this vandalism; half the trees along the paths throughout the woods had been hacked with idiot blaze marks. One day we came upon two young scouts whittling down a cherished dogwood along the pipe line. We told them

# Expanding

they were destroying a protected tree. But they paid no attention. What business was it of ours? Were these our trees?

Just then the scoutmaster came by to inspect the progress, and we repeated our plea. By then the dogwood was seriously maimed.

"It's not a dogwood," pronounced the scoutmaster. "It's an oak. That's O.K. fellas. That'll make a good kettle stick."

The boy scout clearing was kept neat. That was one of the important rules: clean up the camp site before leaving it. But if you walked around the outer perimeter of the clearing, back in the underbrush, you came upon a veritable midden of jars and tin cans and other oddments of boy scout spoor. A complete ring around the camp, at just the distance that a boy could toss a jar. One of us observed that some future archaeologist would find these fairy rings of artifacts a fascinating enigma, and might construct in his imagination some sort of primitive rites, or even an entire culture based upon it.

The boy scouts annoyed us, but we understood their wild exuberance, to be suddenly loosed in this green wilderness. It was the hunters that we hated. The boy scouts whistled and hollered, defaced and defiled, but some of them at least were learning to love the woods. The hunters' presence in the woods was for one purpose only: to destroy. We saw them all year long, sometimes with dogs, sometimes in pairs, but most often alone, and most frequently in the autumn. Stalking down our own trails and pipe lines, shooting at birds and animals we had come to know and think of as our own. We knew they liked to think of themselves as "sportsmen" but we had a poor idea of that; like as not they were hunting protected species, or out of season, or without licenses, or with illegal weapons, or too near road or dwelling. Most often it was ignorance, but also it was knowledgeable cheating. We saw them pot at sitting ducks; we saw them blast at herons; we saw them shoot where there was no chance or effort at retrieval. We heard them tell us they were hunting partridge (no partridge in these woods) with deer rifles (prohibited) in April (out of season) with no license displayed (in fact no license owned). We calculated that one young Nim-

63

rod we came upon was guilty of thirteen simultaneous violations, including the one that we ourselves could have been cited for: trespassing.

When we were older we could dissuade and even turn back some of them with warnings and bluff. Some we harassed by crashing through the woods ahead of them, sending the game scattering in all directions. Some we could never discourage. Their actual toll was probably less than we imagined; a few crows, a few squirrels, a hawk, a heron now and then, rabbits and ducks in fair but never threatening numbers, but much more often tree trunks, signs, tin cans, windows in the waterworks (one day they were shooting the perch that teemed inside an open sump that was part of the drainage system), and if they were lucky, a companion.

We never could understand the lure of it. If it was, as they often said, the pure pleasure of the outdoors, we knew how to partake of it without killing anything. If it was the lure of the quest, the thrill of tracking down, of giving chase, and finally capturing—why, that was a pleasure we experienced many times each day with our binoculars! If it was pride in marksmanship, there were unlimited opportunities with targets and clay pigeons.

We suspected that there were other factors too disturbing to admit: a suspicion of primitive blood lust, of the simple surge of excitement in the act of killing. Perhaps too, an atavistic pride in being once again, even in this so-called civilized world of ours, the food-gathering father figure, the provider from the wilderness, proving his masculinity with a dead duck or a cottontail. For others perhaps it was a relatively safe way to work out repressed aggressions on some helpless surrogate for boss, wife, tax collector, or the world. And for many, it was the simple fascination with the mechanism itself, the polished wood and steel instruments of power that are bought like jewelry, fondled and cleaned and cared for lovingly for far more hours than are ever spent afield. The gun itself demands that it be used.

It outraged us that these hunters had the effrontery to assume for themselves the name of sportsmen. Our idea of a sport was equal combat, matched (or handicapped) opponents, and a total sense of fair play. Carl would say that hunting would only become a sport the day the deer learned how to shoot back. I thought it might truly be a sporting proposition if they could clear all the birds and animals out of a tract of woodland, let all the hunters in together, and let them track and kill each other, with the lone survivor crowned as king of sportsmen. But the hunters twitted with these facetious suggestions looked upon us as lunatics and dangerous fanatics. You cannot, we learned early, josh a hunter about hunting or question his motives. There is an American flag, invisible but ever-present, draped over the shoulder opposite the one that carries the gun. Question the ethics of hunting and you are overwhelmed by patriotism, the Constitution, the pioneer forefathers, defense of family and flag, and the glorious heritage of the American outdoors, with only a momentary pause to blast the wing off a Herring Gull. If you listen long enough, you almost begin to believe that a gun has some other function than to kill. And that killing is the noblest pursuit of mankind.

The woods lured them all in those days. The hunters. The posses of boys racing through, one day as Indians, one day as explorers, one day as knights or pirates or brigands. The boy scouts and their supervised disturbance, the horseback riders, the dog walkers, now and then a pair of lovers or a family on a Sunday walk. The signs that said No Trespassing, or what the shooters left of them, were ignored, except on rare occasions when the Swamp Man, or Old Mr. Quinn from his farmhouse, or the men in the waterworks shooed a few of the intruders off. Who came back, as we did, the very next time they pleased.

It was really not our woods any more, but everyone's woods. But because we were there so much more than anyone, because we were there before dawn and after dark, because we knew and treasured its every trail and every tree, its wildflowers and its animals, its seasons and its scents, so much more intimately than the others, we looked upon them as our own, and all the others as intruders. We were not just woods lovers, we were woods protectors. Although we never spoke of it, or made rules to follow, or ever even consciously reflected on it, we would never break a twig, or pick a flower, or disturb a thicket, or drop a piece of paper, or light a match, or make a racket, or hack a tree within its sacred bounds.

My mother could never understand why I would carry a Baby Ruth wrapper, all the way home from the woods and then drop it on my bedroom floor!

# EIGHT

# Growing

IT WAS JUST AS IF someone had planned and laid out a city not for people but for birds and cottontails and butterflies. In midsummer the roads lay pale and seared, and each step kicked up a little spout of dust that hung on the air and drifted away slowly, like a captive cloud. Ranks of tall wildflowers pressed in from all sides and they were golden, orange, purple, and blue. Dusty Miller, Melilot, Goldenrod, Asters, Thistle, Joe-Pye weed, and in the damp ditches, Tiger Lilies.

At every corner a faded, tilting, half-hidden signpost proclaimed its identity for all the dragonflies to read: Dickens Street, Ibsen Street, Fiske Street, Island Avenue, Forest Avenue, Midfield Road. But at any corner, looking down any street, one could see only a narrow, overgrown track, wide enough for an automobile, and in the distance a gradual merging of the high green walls. On the lesser streets and lanes there was a grassy strip down the center, leaving just the two tire tracks. Here and there, back in the jungle of the blocks enclosed by the streets, one might still see a little sign tacked to a stake or tree, with a lot number on it. Most had bullet holes.

It hadn't been so many years ago, perhaps six or seven, since the roads were cut through this Lord Estate, and the new street signs were erected, and the big auction sale was held out in the meadow on that summer day. The famous auctioneer came down from the city, and the crowd sat on camp chairs under the circus tent, or stood around mopping their faces under the sun, trampling the Oxeye Daisies and Black-eyed Susans. The men were in long shirtsleeves and high collars and straw hats, and the ladies had parasols and fans. The auctioneer bellowed into a megaphone like the one our school cheerleaders used. Some tables had been set up outside the tent for the buyers to go and sign papers.

The prices were high, the people all agreed. The auction sale went on for several days, and in the end all the lots were sold. Everyone knew that real estate was a wonderful investment, and that lots in the suburbs would always increase in value. This was not Florida of recent memory with its boom and bust, its purchases unseen, its underwater swindles. This was beautiful, flat, wooded land—a millionaire's estate! You could buy it with a small down payment and take years to pay.

But then, some of the land proved swampy, and most of it barely above the water table. Times got hard and money disappeared, and suddenly no one was building homes. The people who bought lots on Fiske and Ibsen and Bryant and Howard and Jefferson gave up on the payments or the taxes, defaulted, disappeared, or sold out at a loss. Here and there a house was built and occupied: four or five on all those blocks, and one or two others up in the higher oak woods, but these were large and costly ones, and not really part of the auctioned property. One of these impressive houses was later abandoned; the owner just walked away and left it to the mice and the squirrels, and it stood vacant and going to ruin until a family of squatters moved in one night, living for a while secretly on the second story, but eventually hanging laundry out of the windows as if they owned the place.

The birds and the animals and the weeds never lost the land. Each year they quietly won back more and more of the roads, as if trying to close them altogether and obliterate the whole idea. Sometimes people walked the lanes that were closing up; in certain places culverts under the roads had broken and water flowed across, making it impassable for cars. On Sundays sometimes, a property owner would drive out from the city and stop at Edward and Emerson, or Island and Holmes, or Ibsen and Longacre, and walk in to reassure himself that this property he had invested so rashly in was real, and did exist, and had not vanished into the air. To point to a lot sign from his car, or stumble through the underbrush in search of one, or perhaps even to nail a No Trespassing, Private Property sign to a tree. But the butterflies and the catbirds ignored it, and so did we. Soon, too, it would have a bullet hole or two.

In those days we were the real owners of this property. Often we would stop here, in a detour on the way to the woods, early in the morning when the bird chorus was at its fullest voice. Or we would scuffle along these roads at noon, with the summer heat beating down on our shoulders and the copper butterflies dancing along with us in the dust. Or we would come slowly in the evening, when the thrushes sang from the deeper glens, to put out sugar traps on the tree trunks for moths.

This city of no people, this crisscrossed, abandoned land of field, wood, marsh, and thicket we thought of as an extension of our woods. One of my classmates lived on the edge of the wilderness: we called it "back of Hellers." Often there were birds to be found there when our woods were silent: invisible birds that made the fields chatter and buzz; we were to learn their identities one by one, each a discovery to be celebrated. Sometimes we would come this way on our return from the woods; it was not the shortest way home, but any place without houses and people, with wild things and weeds that grew in jungle profusion, was a better way home.

Then, too, it was another way into the marsh.

Along the eastern edge of the community of no people a road ran north towards the marsh, with the golf course to the east across a deep, wide creek. Here the woods thinned and disappeared in a confusion of cat brier and poison ivy, of goldenrod and ragweed, and here the road turned westward, skirting the marsh, the area a sea of shimmering bulrushes. Half a mile westward you came to another, wider road running north, straight out into the marsh; improbably this one was paved in concrete, although the concrete by then was cracked and broken, weed-grown and neglected. Straight ahead and on both sides was the limitless expanse of salt marsh with, way off to the left, the towers of the city shimmering in the summer heat.

Of all the places we walked in summer, this was the most re-mote and most silent. Under the blue bowl of the sky and the burning sun, with no shade anywhere, nothing stirred and no bird sang. Far out across the marsh, one could see a hawk quar-tering low, now disappearing behind a swell in the sea of rushes, now sliding skywards on spread wings, now reversing himself in a flat sail along some unseen waterway. We knew this hawk—this Marsh Hawk—she was the same one we had seen that first day of the Swamp Man. Somewhere out on those marshes she had nested. Occasionally, almost to emphasize the silence, the marsh echoed to a ringing *chak chak chak chak chak* that seemed to gain in volume and then die away, a hard, harsh protest from some hidden marsh creature. From the ranks of flowers along the road and from the nearby bulrushes, no sound. The whole world seemed muted and hushed under this huge white sun. The keening of the insects had died; the birds, if there were any in the marsh, were sleeping. From the marsh, from the abandoned subdivision we had left, from the decaying railroad trestle far across the salt marsh on the west, from the skies, came only silence. Our voices, strange and foreign in this world suddenly gone lifeless, dried up in our throats. We kicked along the baking concrete that seemed to run out to infinity ahead of us, only our footsteps clacking their uneven rhythm in all that hypnotic world. But the mosquitoes were alive, and they followed us in clouds.

How strange and marvelous it was that everywhere we walked together, somehow we seemed to find new places to explore, roads and paths that no one seemed to use, roads that led us on, farther than we planned to go, luring us beyond the next bend, the next clump of trees, the farthest field. It was exactly like our very lives, curious and fascinating, with each new day an explora-tion, a learning, a discovery, and a turning in the road. Straight roads like this, that reached out to the far horizon, were like dreams, like imagination, leading one further and further along to some unknown destination, some unexpected answer that might be waiting at the end of it.

At last we did come to the end of this road, to the finite answer to the indefinite question. Suddenly there was no more road. It ended simply in a wide sandy place on the edge of a creek as wide as a small pond, with the sea of marsh reaching beyond it for miles. Two Black Ducks sprang upward as we came up to the water's edge and fled with a rush of wings and some loud complaining. Nowhere else was bird, or sign of life, or sound, under that enormous, unreachable, unthinkable, unbounded blue bowl of the sky.

We skipped a few stones across the creek's surface, and then followed a beaten trail around its edge, and so came to an old, rusting water boiler. A big, black iron cylinder with a rusted hole in one end, half buried in the marsh. We straddled it gingerly, for it was fiery hot, tossing pebbles into the creek, looking out to the horizons: silhouetted trestle far to the west, dancing towers of the city beyond it, green expanse of marsh to the north with its towering tree islands, green wall of our woods to the east, and behind us, far along the road we had come, the oaks of the subdivision, now merged in a low blue haze. We sat and slapped mosquitoes, tossed pebbles, played hand games and Indian rassling, pleased at having reached this new *ultima Thule*, thinking of the long walk home. And somehow noticed, scattered on the ground around the rusty boiler, a midden of feathers and bones. We picked them up idly and considered them; many were unknown to us but here surely was the bright epaulet of the red-winged blackbird, and those sky-blue ones might have been from the wing of a duck. Why here? What catastrophe, what enemy, what hunter, what mystery had caused this drift of feathers?

We looked and pondered, and while we looked we kicked our legs against the boiler, swinging our legs the way boys do. And we both heard a furtive rustling inside the metal cylinder. A bird? A mouse? A rat? We jumped down and saw the rusted hole where the boiler pipes had been connected—it was large enough for a rat, or even a cat! We kicked hard and heard the rustling again, and Ted cautiously put an eye up to the hole. No sound. Darkness inside. Then I found a muddy old piece of pipe and swung it mightily against the boiler. CLANG! CLANG! CLANNNGG! Inside the boiler the sound must have reverberated terrifyingly. I paused, and all was silent. CLANG! CLANG! CLANG! We watched the hole. No motion. CLANG! CLANG! CLANG! Whatever beast lived inside that iron drum, it must have been stone deaf by this time. In the end, we gave up. Rattled the pipe inside the boiler and stood up to move away. And just then, at that moment of defeat, a flash of brown fur shot through the hole, scooted, slithered, and almost streaked down into the water—a long, sleek fury animal with a silky, undulant bush of a tail, no less than two feet long, from nose to tail, and rich red brown! Into the creek he slithered, without a sound. Totally submerged but clearly visible a few inches beneath the surface, the fur on his back and tail glistening and rippling in the sunlight, he swam around a bend in the bulrushes and out of sight.

We raced along the shore to intercept him, but he was nowhere to be found. Hiding, no doubt, quite near, nostrils above water, eyes observing us, the rest of him merged with the waters and the bulrush roots, invisible.

All the way home we argued.

"Aw, Ted, you know that was no muskrat. With a big bushy tail like that?"

"But that's the only animal that big that lives out here in the marsh."

"But what's a muskrat doing in a boiler, when you know they make those heapy houses out in the marsh. Anyway, what are all those feathers doing around the hole in the boiler. Do muskrats catch birds?"

"This one does."

"I say he's not a muskrat. No muskrat ever had a bushy tail like that!"

# Growing

"Okay then, know-it-all, what is he?"

"I don't know. Let's look him up in your animal book. Maybe he's a weasel."

"I've never seen a weasel."

"What else is there? A woodchuck?"

"I don't think they swim. Anyway, not under water."

"Whatever he is, let's keep him a secret. And come out here this summer and watch him. Maybe he's got babies and we can catch one and keep it in a cage."

"If he's got babies, you leave them alone. They belong right out there where they live."

"Yeah, I guess so. But I don't like him eating all those birds."

"Well, if that's what he eats, we can't stop him. Except unless you want to kill him."

"I just hope nobody else finds him and kills him. Gee, he was a swell little animal."

"Musky" turned out to be a mink, of course. We walked back to our secret boiler and its treasured occupant again and again that summer, and each time had to deafen him with clanging, then retreat noisily, stand motionless, and wait, before he would dart from the jagged exit and flee to the water. We brought a flashlight and attempted to look into the boiler's inner depths, but saw nothing but a heap of dead vegetation and more feathers. If there was more than one mink living there, we could never verify its presence; the one we did see always seemed to be Musky. His take of birds was wide: Red-winged Blackbirds and grackles and marsh wrens and an occasional duck, and once a Green Heron (with what stealth, surely by night, he had surprised this wide-eyed stalker!). From the fur, bones, and litter around his doorstep, his menu seemed varied: mice, frogs, fish, even grasshoppers. We found his tracks along the muddy banks of the narrower creeks and drainage canals that transected the marsh, sometimes a hundred yards or more from his home; but then, these might have been made by more than a single animal. Musky always looked angry; perhaps *ferocious* is a better word for his untamed, sly, beady-eyed look.

73

# The Lord's Woods

Musk lived there in the boiler undisturbed, except by us, for five years that we knew of, and how many years before that we could not say. Nor did we ever discover what became of him. The iron cylinder rusted away, little by little, and the hole grew larger, and a second one developed in the top. One day when we pounded (our new, adult method of flushing him out was to blow clouds of cigarette smoke in through the hole in the roof) no mink appeared. Several unproductive visits followed, and it was soon evident from the lack of fresh feathers that our little mink was gone.

He could have died a natural death, or moved somewhere else across the marsh. He might have met with hawk or hunter, or ended with one leg jammed in a trap. We never found a trace of him again, or saw his distinctive, circular, four-toed imprints in the mud. Many years later we learned of a man who scratched a living, or supplemented one, by trapping mink around these marshes. Some say that it may still be possible today. But not where Musky lived; that marsh is gone.

All that long and lazy summer we explored our woods and their perimeter, expanding the world we knew; rode our bikes to its edge, then hid them in the jewelweed and continued through on foot. We walked down all its streams, followed all its paths to their endings or meetings, discovered glades here and pools there, marshy patches with cattails in them, a sandy place we called the Cherry Desert, walked along the farm road that skirted the north edge of the woods (years later we would learn that it had a name: Hungry Harbor Road). It was a road to nowhere, winding past a farmhouse at the edge of high oak woods, then cutting through a dense stand of second growth and tangle to a bend where a little red house stood behind one towering spruce tree, in a sea of junk. Whoever lived there—and it seemed to be a man with a disfiguring skin disease and several angry police dogs, fortunately tethered—either dealt in junk or simply had a littered way of life. The magnificent spruce was a landmark at least a century old, common to many of the older farmhouses in the community. They had been imported, it was

# Growing

said, from Norway by an itinerant nurseryman who peddled them, door to door, from his wagon. Beyond the little red house the road wound through more open lands, fields running down to salt marsh, the northern side of that same marsh we had penetrated walking to Musky's home. Later, we discovered, this same road, filled with huge potholes, ruts, and almost impassible puddles, snaked all the way across the marsh, crossed the abandoned railway trestle and eventually joined the distant turnpike that was the far western boundary of the salt marsh.

Although we invented our own names for the topographic features of our world, more as a convenience than the just due of the explorer, others before us had exercised these rights, and the most prominent features of the landscape had already been named. Unknown to us, the wide stream at the northern edge of the woods was Foster's Brook or Mott Creek, depending on which map you consulted. Its upper end was of disputed nomenclature, apparently, while the lower end that ran through the salt marsh to the bay was always called Mott, or Mott's Creek.

We called the other major stream Teal Stream and did not learn for thirty years that it had been named Doxey's Brook long before we were born. That summer we explored its entire length, past Three Bridges, the Stone Bridge, Stepping Stone Island, and out into the marsh, discovering there a fine, wide swimming hole with a tiny sandy beach, shaded by one stunted cherry tree covered with poison ivy, remote, invisible except to hawks and swallows. Beyond the swimming hole Teal Stream slid westward again and joined Foster's Brook, deep in the salt marsh. And there, intriguing and mysterious, tilted up on mud and marsh, burned out, but still identifiable, its huge bolts and nails rusting into skeletons, lay the barge.

How it came this far upstream, on what wings or unimaginable high tide, to become lodged and abandoned miles from deep water, we never could understand. But we wove a story around it, as we did with all our landmarks: Washington's Barge, we called it. Used to smuggle guns to the rebels who were working underground in Tory-held Long Island during Revolutionary days. Brought in on a high tide from Jamaica Bay by night, stranded there in the morning, its cargo delivered along the secret paths of our woods and others that joined in a network across the island. Then, years later perhaps, burned when the marshes burned, as they did every spring. We knew, of course, from Mr. Perry's history course that the Loyalists had held tightly to Long Island throughout the Revolution and until 1783, after that disaster to Washington on Prospect Hill, but we knew too that there had been rebel activity behind the lines and this barge had played a part! Why, Mr. Hewlett down the street was a direct descendant of a Tory colonel, Richard Hewlett, and he was a spy too; my father insisted that descendants of anti-independence ancestors should never have been granted the right to vote, for they tended to vote Tory still.

That summer too we moved our boundaries outward, Carl and I, or Ted and I, or Johnny and I. Now we had defined our woods and knew what was beyond it on all sides: farms to the north, marsh to the west, our village to the south, and grassy fields across Mill Road to the east. Not, as we had first thought, trackless wilderness in all directions, but more like a spreading sanctuary surrounded, eventually, by places with people in them, people who knew little and cared less about this place we loved. Some knew it as the Lord's Woods, but most called it, if they knew of it at all, the Waterworks Property, or Woodmere Woods.

There was no pressure on the woods in those earliest years of ours. Each of the suburban communities around us was a compact, tailored island unto itself, surrounded and separated from its neighbor by a green belt of farms, fields, and woodlands. The marshes were untouched and unspoiled, except for the flat ditched meadows where the salt hay was harvested. Now and then, as we were growing up, a new house would appear on one of the vacant plots to be found on almost every block even in the heart of the village, or perhaps an entire street of houses somewhere on the edge of town. But our woods were inviolate; the Lord Estate was languishing; soon even the golf course was abandoned. We roamed them all now almost as our private domain; rode our bikes too to more distant hunting grounds: the

# Growing

creeks and marshes along the bay at the southern edge of the village, the marshes and ponds beyond the farms to the north, the beaches across the inlet where we could look out across the ocean, all the way to Spain!

One of our pastimes of that summer was the aquarium. I had acquired an old tank somewhere, and so had my two friends and classmates Johnny and Beano. Together the three of us made a series of expeditions into the woods, hung with bottles and dip nets. Sprawled along the banks of Teal Stream and stripped to the waist, we would lie in wait for killifish, or water striders, or any fresh-water life we could find. Now chasing whirligig beetles across the surface of the brook, now delving deep into the muddy bottom to come up with a giant water beetle, a crazy diving water beetle, or a treasured back swimmer. We took them all: nymphs of dragonflies and caddis flies, tadpoles in all stages of development, once even a prized baby pickerel. Brought them home (some died from the rough ride home on the bicycle), emptied bottles and jars into the tank that stood on my window-sill, watched fascinated as beetles, each with a taillight bubble of air, zoomed in wild arcs across the tank. The surface bugs—water striders and whirligigs—died first. Others lingered, to succumb to natural causes or the rampant cannibalism that cannot be controlled in a single small tank. The more aggressive beetles, the back swimmers, and the tadpoles thrived for a while, as the algae flourished in the sunshine and the water turned the color of pea soup. Eventually, as they usually do, the aquarium died and was carried out and emptied, much to the relief of Eliza, who loathed that bug-filled, stinking brew—only to be filled again the following summer. But it had added another dimension to the world around us.

The woods! A green, gold, scarlet, multicolored wonder of a world, ancient and yet ever-changing, constant and yet filled with surprises, setting for dreams and fantasies, schoolroom without books, a sanctuary for birds and mammals, fish and crawling things, bugs and boys. Beautiful in every aspect and in every week of the year, and more prized because it was at once so accessible and so remote from the outside world. We had no words in those days to say how we felt about the Lord's Woods, but we cherished them. They were truly at the center of our existence.

# NINE

# Autumn

THERE IT WAS AGAIN! We stood on the Cinder Road where it crossed Teal Stream and craned our necks upward at the sound. The winds of autumn had torn holes in the roof of our secret summer world. Shards of sunlight showered down, splintering on leaves that shivered and danced and spun around us in swirls of gold and copper.

Somewhere up in that incredibly deep, clean, azure sky a bird was screaming: his high-pitched half-whistle piercing the air between us. The scream came again, much nearer now, from the north, and then a moment later the big hawk wheeled into view, high overhead, screaming as he flew. There he is! we cried together and watched as dark wings sailed on invisible billowings of air; we ran along the road under the willows to hold him in our sight as he sailed across the sky, now flapping, now soaring, circling back to give us a second look. Long wings, black above when he wheeled, creamy white below with shoulder smudges and perhaps some black around the face. Hey, look at that! In one talon, held straight out, a little orange fish! One moment later and he was gone, down across Stepping Stone Island and out towards the marsh. Hey, you know what that was? I said. My first Fish Hawk! And out came the pocket guide, dirtier and more dog-eared than ever, confirm it.

# The Lord's Woods

We watched and listened for his return but he was gone, moving southward with the season, stopping by creek or pond to plunge down for his prey, a flash of black and white against the blue, like a hallucination that appeared and was gone almost before you were were aware of it. Southward he sailed on the first northwest wind of the week, flashing his black-and-white wings against the sky, piping his shrill challenge on the rolling air, gone where, and how far?

We went back to the bridge and talked about him, the clean, quick, perfect image of him sailing across our vision like a blessing, or a gift. And we lay face downward on the concrete railing of the bridge and peered into the sky-blue water that was dark beneath the blue. Deep down there long green strands of algae were beginning to brown, like the leaves that floated over them. Tiny brown killifish, almost invisible, darted here and there, reacting to each leaf that fell, each shadow that passed, moving sometimes in unison, sometimes in little explosions to whatever fright, or whim, or secret signal moved them.

We wondered how it was they moved together; who decided which way to go, and how it told the others. We watched, but in that little school of killies we could see no leader, could hear no sound, could find no clue to this mystery. Now they idled in sunlight, a fraternity at rest; now they streaked away together, a posse in flight to the darkness under the bridge. We thought they moved in concert because they had no brains or initiative, and since each was identical, whatever moved one of them moved them all. (It seemed possible to us then, and now forty years later, no one has put forward a better theory.)

Along the steep banks of Teal Stream the weeds and flowers, now rank and dusty, their greens turned gray, seed heads where flowers had flared, shook in the wind. Last night's frost had crumpled some of the shoots that still were green and tender; they wore a damaged, blackened, sickened look. They were dying.

The wind sprang, a shower of leaves flew, and from somewhere in the bracken nearby, the sounds of small birds moving and conversing joined the rustle and sighing of the leaves. A

80

thrush stood suddenly on a log, alert, and looked at us, then silently flew down and away. A little kindergarten of kinglets came through, pell-mell, taking frantic possession of the locust by the stream bank, then the sweet gum, then the willow. Talking to themselves in high, thin sibilants, saying *Seeee! Seee! Seee!*

A cottontail came down the path, lalluping along, nose quivering, then stopped, frozen and almost invisible in the clutter of leaves around him. Bud swung one arm upward and he shot away, scooting over the ground, then stopped to watch us from behind a tall brown fern. A towhee called, one momentary echo of spring. And then gave the field over to the wind.

All was silent again for a long moment, and then a surprise! Around the bend in the stream, swimming down from Three Bridges, came two graceful ducks, a companionate pair, keeping their heads close together, now pausing to delve into the weeds below the surface, now venturing ahead with wheeling hesitation. Small, sleek, with pinkish-brown backs and sides, one with blue head and white crescent moon on the face. Not Blue-winged Teal! Not here, swimming in Teal Stream! We watched motionless, scarcely breathing, as they moved closer. Then suddenly, at no signal we could discern, they sprang into the air and wheeled off across the cattail marsh, flying low, keeping close, making no sound.

As we lay watching our world, a new sound crowded in above the wind; a man-made noise, a blatant motor noise that barked and sputtered, whining above the trees. Through the windows in the leaves, across the sky, moved that marvelous machine, a little biplane painted red and white, with black numbers on the wings. It moved slowly against the wind, not very far above the trees, its wires and struts shining in the sun, the luminous disk against the nose all that could be seen of the propeller.

It was still a miracle, the little flying machine. None of us had yet flown, or knew anyone who had. Not so long ago Lindbergh had thrilled the world with his flight from Long Island to Paris—right from the same Roosevelt Field where my father sometimes took us on Sundays to look at the airplanes, watch them fly, see them stunting and parachuting, and where we would beg, unsuccessfully, to be taken on a ride: once around the field was only $2.oo!

We knew where the little biplane came from. If you kept on walking down the Old Gray Road, it wound through farm fields for a mile or more, crossing two deep streams, then forking right, past a scattering of houses, and coming to a row of wooden sheds whose open doors revealed a fascination of airplanes. Biplanes like the Jenny overhead, stubby little monoplanes with round noses, strange fat-bodied birds with closed cabins, even one triplane, half-assembled, lacking tail and motor. Out on the grass behind the sheds were more planes, tethered like hawks against storm or theft, and beyond them the vast grassy expanse of the flying field. All along its near edge it came down to farms and marshes; on the far side, a mile away, was the main highway. They called it Curtiss Field.

Though we marveled at the little biplane then, the droning noise of the engines would come to plague us later as the field grew in activity and the sky filled with students, sightseers, test pilots, and even the U.S. Navy, wheeling ever-noisier machines above our heads and out across our farms, our marshes, fields, and woods. Sometimes we would be forced to stand and wait and use up all our cuss words before the drone would fade away (though it seemed to linger forever in the ears) and we could hear the warbler in the tree. It didn't seem fair that they could so easily take possession of what was ours. But sometimes, enviously, we wished we were up there with them, veering around the boundless sky.

We walked on through the woods along the Cinder Road, then cut across the Pipe Farm by the waterworks, into the birch grove before we heard the shouting and the laughter. There were kids in Bare Ass Beach, the deep sand pit with the water at the bottom of it, the one that Carl and I had discovered and had skipped stones into, years before. Swimming, on this windy day in mid-October! We recognized them all: one or two were friends and the rest we knew by name. The smallest one, Sammy, stood shivering and naked on the edge and shouted to Peter, who was splashing in the middle. Two other boys, the browns of summer sun still staining them from head to toe, were wrestling on the bank, trying to push each other in. Johnny and Chee were drying themselves with their shirts behind a birch clump up the bank. Every one of them hailed us with loud greetings and insisted that the water was warm, the swimming fine, and that down in the hollow of B.A.B. there was no edge to the wind.

There was no wind down in the bowl of B.A.B. The sun was weakly warm. The water was numbing, paralyzing, and as we waded in, a shock to loins and belly. We splashed across the hole and back and scrambled out, in time to watch one shoe go flying into the very center of the dark brown water and sink from sight. I yelped and went for Sammy, who held my other shoe aloft and who managed to sink it also, though he got for his trouble a bloody lip. When the shoes stopped flying and the laughter died, Peter, who seemed impervious to the icy waters, retrieved three of them, but five were lost forever. Then the whole gang together, warmed by combat and by the secret delight at having participated in this outrageously forbidden rite, walked to their bikes barefoot, the pleasure only vaguely tempered by the problem of explaining the lost shoe, the wet shirt, the muddy legs, and the damp, though still-legible, pocket guide to the birds. Beano confided to me later that some girls we knew had been watching us from behind the birch grove, but I never believed him. I knew those girls and they could never have witnessed the skirmish of the flying shoes without saying something about it later, and they never mentioned it, or even hinted at it in that silly giggling way girls have.

I caught a little bit of hell about the shoe, and a pretty good cold. That was all. But that October day—Columbus Day—was the day we saw the Fish Hawk!

That fall I joined the club. One evening I was invited to a meeting as a guest and then shortly afterward, was elected to the rank of Associate Member and welcomed into the little fraternity of boys who had joined to form, a year or two before, the Bird Club. It was another year before I earned full membership.

The club met every Friday evening during the school year in

a little low-ceilinged room in Roy's father's basement. An assortment of castoff chairs, some of them still-comfortable wicker porch furniture, others hard and straight-backed, were arranged around the walls. At one end a large table held our library of books and magazines and a few exhibits: nests, eggs, and feathers. A rather badly stuffed, one-eyed Saw-whet Owl hung from a wire in one corner, and a few nests in their original branches hung from pipes and odd projections. An ancient, threadbare Oriental rug carpeted the cement floor; an Audubon bird chart and a few dusty prints adorned the walls. One floor lamp of ancient vintage and one overhead light provided a dim but intimate atmosphere. Behind the thin wood partition the oil burner was subject to fits of roaring activity, but it repaid us by providing a feeling of snug sanctuary on bitter winter nights.

Friday was Bird Club Night, and every member was required to attend every meeting. To be excused from attendance, you had to be really sick (and Roy's father was the village doctor) or have an irrevocable, imperative conflict, and no mere social engagement was irrevocable or imperative. The proceedings were formal (more or less) and the discourse serious (more or less), allowing for our ages and natural exuberance. Each of us had committee assignments and on each of us in turn devolved the most important committee charge: refreshments. Which meant bringing the cookies and soft drinks that by ancient tradition followed the meetings.

I rang the doorbell at Roy's big brick house about five minutes to eight, carefully washed and combed (Roy's house was on our block, next door to Carl's and I could dash through Old Lady Richardson's to get there), and was ushered by Delia through the kitchen to the cellar stairs to join the group already filling the little cellar room with noisy conversation. The meetings began when Mr. Harrower arrived. Dave was our guiding spirit: the fiery-tempered, irascible, lovable biology teacher whose idea this club was. Dave was a rough taskmaster in class, and roughest of all on his Bird Club boys; no one could ever accuse him of favoritism. To the rest of the student body he was, respectfully, Mr. Harrower. Only seniors and members of the Bird Club (away from school) were permitted the familiarity of the first name, and we prized the honor. By some schoolmates we were even called, enviously perhaps, Dave's Boys.

We could hear his measured tread at the top step, and by the time he reached the clubroom, we were all quiet and seated in our places. Dave paused at the door, thumbs hooked in his belt, rocked once or twice on his toes, surveyed the room and each of us with feigned distaste, proceeded with measured strides across the room to the most comfortable wicker armchair in the corner, sat himself down, crossed his legs, drew carefully on his slim cigar, flicked the ash into the waiting ashtray, then slowly broke into a broad smile, proclaiming, "All right, gentlemen, let us proceed."

Roy was president, of course. Not just because the clubroom was in his cellar. He was the oldest boy, by a single year, and he was the natural choice. A good birder, he was also an expert moth and butterfly collector and had spent the last two summers collecting for the Museum of Natural History in the city. Slim, lean of jaw, with a tousle of rusty hair and penetrating blue eyes, Roy was intense, articulate, and sharp-tongued, but always gentle. He could destroy your most precious, ill-considered hypothesis with a single pointed question and a shy, apologetic smile.

Next to Roy sat Bob, doing his best to conceal a most prodigious ability. Clipped of speech and saturnine of appearance, Bob was a theoretician at fifteen, blessed with an incredible memory and a native quickness at learning that astonished and dismayed us all. Bob could quickly master problems while we still struggled with them and then grow quietly helpful as he explained them to us, without too much show of impatience. With Bob, as with Roy, went an air of quiet authority: you contradicted either of them at your peril. Bob asked many questions; he could lead you through an intricate line of logic and then leave you at the point of obvious revelation with a wide grin of triumph. Bob lost few arguments.

Across the room from Bob sat his younger (by two years) brother Ben, the one who had warned us that first day not to pick the Arbutus. Ben was supercharged, aggressive, extroverted,

# The Lord's Woods

noisy, and bright. As brilliant as Bob was, some said, but involved in so many school activities, in sports and birds and music and school government and whatnot that his school record was a mess. Like Bob, Ben had a shock of wild black hair and dark eyes with a twinkle in the corners of them. Ben quarterbacked the junior football team with total recklessness, sang with the school band, and when, some years later, in a moment of quickly rescinded rashness the club appointed a Lady's Auxiliary (Roy's kid sister Natalie and Andy's sister Nancy), Ben was the Lady's Auxiliary Committee.

Howie, our secretary, sat next to Roy and was another type entirely. Howie had wavy, sandy hair brushed straight back, small, neat, regular features with a pointed chin, a rather prim and proper look, and a pedantic way of speaking. Howie worked hard at everything he did in an orderly way; though small of stature, he was quick and light on his feet and a good athlete. Not one to make a lot of fuss or noise, Howie was sometimes the but of gentle raillery, perhaps just for his serious, purposeful manner. Howie took it in smiling good grace; we were all good friends and we secretly admired his total dedication to excellence.

Next to Howie, and crowding him with elbow and knee, sprawled Richard, whom we all called Duke. This was the big, awkward, unpredictable, thunderingly noisy, and excitable odd man of the club. Duke had the loudest voice, the most explosive laugh, the slouchiest walk, the most enormous feet, and the most questioning mind of all of us, but it was a mind cluttered with unsorted facts and unresolved theories, unrelated facts and uncontrolled emotions. It was Duke who would, more than once, cave in my mother's best unholstered chair by collapsing into it. ("Doesn't that boy ever sit down like other people?") It was Duke who would clear the platter of cookies with one sweep of a giant fist, or gulp a hot dog in two bites, or stay up all night struggling (and failing to decipher) a Schopenhauer text someone had recommended. Duke absorbed a constant and unrelenting kidding, often cruel, as boys can be, about his horse-faced look, his gangling gait, his awkwardness. You couldn't walk down a path

86

next to Duke without being bumped. If he jumped a creek, he fell backward into it. If he rode his bike, it would crash into a tree. Once he said, quite politely, "Pardon me," to a post he had stumbled into, and for months we all excused ourselves elaborately to posts, trees, gates, and each other. Duke was Howie's age: one year younger than Roy, but in my class. Bob was exactly my age, but one year ahead of me, in Howie's class.

On opposite sides of the room sat the twins, Daniel and Finley. Daniel, whom we called Buddy, or Bud, was solid, stocky, broad of shoulder and face, with a shock of lank, yellow corn silk for hair, blue eyes, and a droll manner. Bud affected a twang from down-East Maine, where the family summered; he was our actor, mimic, and jester but a serious devotee of our woods. Finley, or just Finny, was Bud's younger brother by fifteen minutes, it was said, but no one would believe that they were twins, or even brothers. Bud was broad and blond and stocky; Finny was our tallest member, dark-haired, angular, narrow-faced, and taciturn. Finny went along, not for any real dedication to birds or wild-life, but just because that was where Buddy and all their friends were. Finny didn't pay too much attention to the more abstruse aspects of our conversation. Often he seemed to be miles away, or not anywhere at all. Finny could be witty and fun; he could be, like Buddy, quick-tempered (and equally quick to cool). His major claim to fame was the beautiful purple hue his hands assumed in cold weather and his constant colds, but most of all, his fantastic capacity for sleep. You always knew what Fin was doing if he wasn't visible: he was asleep. Sometimes he was both visible and asleep.

Finally, between Finny and me sat Tommy, Howie's kid brother, who had been honored with a special category all his own—Junior Member. Tommy was two years younger than Ben, round-faced and eager, quiet and respectful. He had no fear of asking questions in his high-pitched voice; his knowledge, as he walked everywhere at Howie's side, and his confidence was slowly growing. Tommy's normal role was that of listener.

"O.K. Meeting come to order! Secretary, call the roll!"

From Howie, in the corner, "Roy!"

# The Lord's Woods

"Here!"

From Ben, "Aw, come on, Roy, we're all here."

"Duke?"

"Here."

"Bud?"

"Present."

"Fin? Fin! Hey, Fin!"

"Yeah."

"Bibs?"

"Here."

"Tommy?"

"Here!"

"All present, Mr. President." The secretary then read the minutes of the last meeting, duly reporting that all had been present, that Andy and Allan had been discussed as candidates for membership (tabled), that the idea of an annual publication of the club would be looked into, and if it seemed feasible (Dave to look into the financing since the treasury held $7.45), we would start work on it promptly, which meant that each member would consider writing an article, long or short. That the club would hold its first formal Christmas Census on December 27, with more details to be decided later. The paper of the evening by Bob had been a discussion of the finches that are likely to visit in winter. Birds recorded during the week included four Pigeon Hawks at the beach, a Pied-billed Grebe in the bay, and several species of warblers in the woods.

The minutes approved, Bud and Ben, with Duke supplying asides, then described the sensational trade they had effected to augment the club library and club treasury. Iggy, the pet Herring Gull, was gone. Iggy had been found broken-winged one morning in September along the water's edge at the beach, and Bud and Ben had carried him home (riding a bike with a struggling gull in one's arms takes a certain talent, mostly for falling off unharmed), but Iggy, recovering on expensive table tidbits and canned fish, had outworn his welcome at Ben's house, at Bud's house, and was now nowhere welcome at all. But, thanks to the unsuspected gullomania discovered in the person of one Johnny L., the unwelcome gull proved negotiable, and the club treasury was richer by two dollars, a pair of guinea pigs, and a somewhat worn and tattered (front cover missing) but massive copy of Studer's *Birds of America*. The sale, or barter, was approved with cheers.

"How'd you ever make this deal?" asked Howie, as we crowded around to examine the newly acquired Studer.

"He was obviously gullible," answered Roy, with a grin.

"He was guileless too," added Bob.

"We Igged him on," contributed Bud.

"He needed a gull friend," was my contribution.

"O.K., that's enough," squelched the president. "Everybody sit down. Dave, any news about the annual? And chance of getting any money?"

"We could go into the broken-winged gull business," roared Duke. "The treasury is now $9.45."

Dave explained that he thought he could talk the school administration into a little fund for publication and perhaps a printer (he knew a few) might contribute part of the cost, if we produced something worthwhile. We'd better get started, because these things took a lot of time. Each of us should choose a subject we knew something about, and after we all had subjects the club approved, we had to collect our data and then write. We would need some short articles, too, and other features like the club's bird list for the year, and news items.

"What are we going to call it?"

A chorus of voices responded with suggestions. (We had been asked to think about a name, which unquestionably had to be a bird name, since all the famous journals were named after birds.) The Hawk? The Tern? The Gull? (No! No!) The Gannet? The Sandpiper? (Hey, that's not bad!) The Heron? In the end, it came down to a vote between the Herons and the Egrets, and the Herons won. There was no publication anywhere, as far as we knew, named *The Heron*, and how could anyone find a more appropriate name for a publication about the birds of our

89

water-coursed, marsh-margined world? "In fact," Duke prom-, ised, "I'm going to write my article about the herons of Long Island; we've seen ten different species this year."

Andy and Allen having been disposed of—we decided to invite them to a few meetings and bird walks as a trial—now came the paper of the evening, "The Skeleton of Birds." I carefully unrolled my notes and drew from the shoe box I had brought the mounted pigeon skeleton I had borrowed from the school's biology lab. I pointed out the bones, starting with the skull, helped here and there by Dave on pronunciation and corrected now and then by Roy on identification. But when I finished, a half an hour later, with damp brow and a tight chest, there was a round of applause and a "Thank you, Bibs, good job," from the president, and only then I realized that everyone had listened, even Finny, and no one had interrupted with jokes. But I vowed never again to forget the name of that little hole in the skull the spinal cord runs through—that darned occipital condyle. And I never did.

Tommy had seen a Yellow-bellied Flycatcher over in the Lord Estate, but his identification didn't stand up under the merciless cross fire of Roy and Bob, even with Howie defending. Duke's snow white grackle was noted and discussed, and Duke was assigned to give the next paper, on albinism in birds. Bob and Ben reported a flight of thrushes on the seventeenth. Our Fish Hawk (let's call it Osprey from now on) was accepted without surprise and with no mention of the swimming incident. And Fin reported, to an uproar of derision, that Mr. Hudson had told him he had seen a Ferruginous Rough-legged Hawk and a Le Conte's Sparrow in the woods on Thursday. Mr. Hudson was a dedicated and serious bird watcher of sorts, who wore rather shabby clothes, carried a pair of two-power opera glasses and a little notebook, and whom we encountered from time to time in almost every haunt. In his notebook he inscribed in pencil the birds as he saw them, and they were always incredible. We liked Mr. Hudson, but how could you see a Lark Bunting, a Mountain Bluebird, and a Cory's Least Bittern all in one day on Long Lsland? We always wondered whether Mr. Hudson

believed he was seeing those impossible birds or whether he
wrote them down in his notebook just to impress us, and whether
he thought we believed them. We never questioned him to his
face, accepting his reports with feigned excitement that seemed
to please him. In the end, we decided that he did indeed believe
his fantastic records and that he was absolutely nutty; I mean,
how could anyone make such mistakes? (I had made a few like
that only a year ago and now hastened to erase them from my
records.) Mr. Hudson fell from grace when Duke brought
him home from the woods to dinner one night and he borrowed
five dollars from Duke's father and never paid it back; in fact, he
was never seen again. (The official ornithological archives of the
region carry no records by any Mr. Hudson, if that was his
name, and he and his dreams have long since passed into obliv-
ion.)

At last, with a flourish, the meeting was adjourned, and Duke
went to get the refreshments he had brought. The tray of cherry
sodas was brought down, amid much complaining that only
Duke liked cherry soda, the boxes of cookies were torn open
and demolished, and we crowded around Dave to ask about the
census and to look at the Studer. It was an elaborate, pretentious,
and totally third-rate work, but worth a hungry gull or two
in anybody's market. And before we broke up to shout good
nights and seek our separate ways home through the gusty,
moon-frosted night, we'd got Dave to talking about the Costa
Rican jungle, where he'd searched for ancient Indian artifacts.
Decided who would get the guinea pigs. Cleaned up the room,
carried the tray with empty glasses upstairs, straightened the
piles of magazines, and arranged to meet tomorrow morning, at
my house, and walked around the edge of the bay with Duke
and Bud and maybe, if he could rouse himself from bed that
early, his twin brother.

So it was every Friday evening through those years, with the
boys growing older and going off to college and a few new boys
joining; Dave sitting in his corner chair, rolling the cigar between
thumb and first finger, quietly questioning, guiding, drawing us
onward and outward to grow and to mature. Those Friday

evenings in Roy's cellar were an extension of our days in the woods; the little room was an indoor extension of the woods themselves, the place where the week's discoveries were sorted out, discussed, confirmed, and made a part of the record. They were too the essence of companionship; each of us as close to all the others as brothers; each welcome in all the other houses (and Dave's house, too) at any hour or for any meal; building our friendship slowly in the only lasting way: shared experience. With early morning forays into the woods, across the marshes, to the beaches and the bays and the creeks that flowed into them, to the fields and farmlands and more distant ponds and marshes, and later, first in Dave's car and then by our parents' cars (loaned with trepidation and silent prayers), to farther shores and even wider horizons, to add new insights to our expanding knowledge.

But always, the heart of it for all of us, the spiritual home and the essential classroom, the secret wellspring that we cherished above all others, was the Lord's Woods.

# TEN

# Winter

THE SNOW had begun drifting down some time after midnight; I could sense it as I lay in bed, quilted to the nose, hearing the hush overcoming all outdoor sounds. Even the one car that came slowly down the street sounded as if it were wrapped in cotton and it faded out of hearing long before it reached the corner. Now and then an insistent flurry of snowflakes would pepper the windowpane, but I was asleep again before it happened more than twice. Sometime later I was vaguely aware that my mother was in the room, a white wraith, seeing to the windows as she always did when there was a storm, gone again with the enfolding gray drifts of sleep.

By morning the whole visible world was clean and new, lying silent, wrapped in a veil that shrouded the earth, the sky, the nearest houses, and every tree, branch, and twig. Even the telephone wires hung like gauzy garlands; the golden horse weather vane at the peak of Hewlett's barn had a snowy mane. It was a world compressed, foreshortened, with no distant horizon, with only the nearby visible. Below, all the lawns, gardens, sidewalks, and the street were a single unbroken white, like one continuous community lawn.

No time to stand shivering at the open window. Now, out

there, to be submerged, surrounded, immersed, and smothered in that enveloping white! In an hour or less the village plow would scrape down the middle of the street, leaving a wide black scar. People and dogs would soon be abroad, defacing the purity of the scene with their own random wanderings. If the sun came out, the snow on the evergreens, on the maple branches, on roofs and wires and every rhododendron leaf would melt or blow away, leaving only a sullied ground of all that miracle of white.

There was only one place to be now, before it all vanished. I pulled on my clothes and boots—toothbrush and comb could wait—and ran out, ducking behind the garage, getting a faceful of snow in the privet hedge, loped across Old Lady Richardson's lawn for the thousandth time. Bob and Ben were already up and dressed, urged on by the same wordless imperative. We stomped across the tennis courts, down the middle of the boulevard, angled across the school grounds, and entered the white lace tunnel of the Cinder Road. A single croaking jay let us in, complaining like a concierge.

The storm had left six or seven inches of snow on the ground before it moved off, but the air was still heavy with the crisp scent of more. The sky, through snow-hung branches, was a pale fog gray, and in the cold winter light the trunks of the maples receded in ranks of melancholy black. Only mists of catbrier gave glaucous shading to the scene.

By the Indian Tree we detoured, then paused to look down into the waters of Jewelweed Stream. The last two weeks of January had been mild (the January thaw, old Ed Brower, the ancient bayman, had called it and told us we could expect one every winter; he could remember back to 1860 and every January brought one warm week, you could be certain of it). Down there flowing water, like liquid black crystal, spun down between ice and snowdrift.

There at the stream's edge by the Indian Tree we discovered that we were not the first to come this way today. Here was a constellation of clear footprints, as if some animal had come to drink, and then we found a line of prints, spaced evenly but meandering along a path of their own, a trail that ventured through the snow-heaped underbrush and off into the woods.

We crouched over the tracks and considered them excitedly. Rabbit? Squirrel? Weasel? Or possibly a skunk? A cat perhaps? A dog?

"I think the paw marks are too big for a little animal like a squirrel," I ventured.

"But what kind of a bigger animal would hole up in that thicket?" Ben asked.

"Maybe one of those wild house cats that live in the woods in summer holes up in a hollow tree somewhere."

"Aw, for Pete's sake, how could he live? Cats don't hibernate. They have to eat every day."

"I think it's a rabbit."

"Naw," Ben said, "a cottontail shows you a double track and a tail mark, and the big part of the hind leg where they almost sit down each time they hop. This track was made with one paw being carefully set down, one after the other, and it must have been an animal with long legs."

"How far are those prints apart? Can you measure it?"

"Longer than my shoe, and I'm size seven. I guess it's a little bit less than a foot. Eleven inches, at the most."

"You know what I bet?" from Bob, and we both looked up at him expectantly. Whatever Bob had deduced was worth serious consideration. "A fox. A little red fox. It had to be a pretty good-sized animal, right? Or some part of its belly would have touched the snow. It can't be a cat or a dog, living out here in winter. Any kind of squirrel or rabbit would have a long paw, not a round one like this. O.K.? So what else is there? Maybe a skunk, but I say fox anyway."

"That's no skunk," I insisted. "They have a hand-shaped print. The front paws do, anyway. We had one in a cage one summer up at Sacandaga. This is no skunk. Anyway, skunks kind of shuffle along. They'd mess up the snow all around."

Ben was excited now. We all were. A red fox? *A red fox!* None of us had ever seen one in our woods. How was it, with all those countless days we came here and played here, we had never seen sign of fox, until this silent, wintry moment with its indelible evidence?

We stomped and beat around the thicket for a while, to no avail, then walked along the Cinder Road, considering the mystery of the fox. I wanted to go home and look up fox tracks in my mammal book, but I wanted to walk through this woven white fabric of a snow-clean world even more.

At the little cattail marsh by the willows we stopped again to search for footprints. Here, most certainly, was a cottontail or two. They'd come up from the other side of Teal Stream, where the Pink Lady's-Slipper bloomed in May, and had crossed over the Stone Bridge and headed down toward Stepping Stone Island. But even before they had appeared another much smaller animal had come this way; his tiny tracks were almost full of drifted snow, and we could not make them out. Surely a rodent, perhaps a gray squirrel or a muskrat. But a muskrat would leave a long wavering median line with its tail.

The hush at the heart of the woods was complete; we stood and succumbed to its spell. Our own breathing was all we heard; the world was wrapped in white insulation and we were all stone deaf. For some reason, even the thumping of the pumps was inaudible. Perhaps they were not pumping today. And yet the woods in winter, even at this evanescent moment of perfection, was not the secret, hidden place of summer. Here in late January all her secrets were laid bare, her shadowy Indian trails exposed and naked, her aisles of trees standing unclothed and unprotected; all mystery gone, the last of the clinging oak leaves down and buried, and all that life that teemed in her in summer asleep, or dormant, or dead. The secret woods now open and defenseless against any wind, any prying eye, and ourselves so much nearer to the sky.

Walking home, we were pleased to find two chickadees picking around the catkins of a birch, talking to each other, and Bob, who could whistle as high as the chickadee song, had them answering him excitedly. We heard one crow go overhead, recognizing our presence with a kind of frosty *caaahh*, not so much in anger as to let us know who owned what.

(The days that followed that first morning would never be quite as pristine. The second day might be better, if the snow melted and compacted a little, for finding animal tracks, particularly those of the tiny animals, but our own footprints and the tracks of other visitors, the clutter of snowball fights and of rolling around in the snow, and of leaping, snuffling dogs would sully this all-but-untouched scene. And of course the snow would come blowing or melting from the twigs and branches. The bramble thicket, now a tapestry of curving white plumes, would become merely brambles again; the interwoven whites of branches would become a haze of grays and blacks. A wind would come up, and the endless creaking and complaining of the trees would begin again. The snow would stay pure white for a day or two, and then the chimney's sooty streamers would drift down and sully it, and it would begin to look old and worn, patched and torn.)

Where the woods came to an end by the white farmhouse, we paused once more. No one had stirred that morning; not even the big dog was to be seen. The three tall spruces in the yard were heavy with snow, every branch bending low. We stared up into the trees, as we always did with evergreens. And we all saw it—the three of us—at the very same instant! A dark, vague lump next to the trunk, about thirty feet up.

"Hey, there's an owl!"

"A long-eared!"

Of course, Bob named it first. The Long-eared Owl was perched, looking down at us from a snow-banked hollow in the branches. His ears straight up, his body stretched tall and narrow and leaning outward to watch us, and his eyes big and round, amber aggies. Blinking, now and then, slowly, with what seemed to be the greatest disdain.

We pounded each other and whispered congratulations, standing below the tree, trying to see if there were other owls hidden there, for we had heard that sometimes Long-eared Owls roosted in evergreens in family flocks. Finding no others, we watched him as intently as he watched us; to memorize his soft, streaked plumage, the dark-ringed face pattern, the tiny beak almost hidden, the powerful talons gripping the branch. He was our first owl in the woods; one day that same spring we found a Barn Owl in a tall maple not fifty yards away.

Then we raced up Westwood Road, across the school grounds, across the tennis courts to Dave's house, to bring the tidings. To look at the splendid color plates by Fuertes in Dave's new book on the birds of Massachusetts, the best we had ever seen. (Yes, he was indeed a Long-eared, no doubt whatsoever.) To consider where he had come from: what northern pine forest had been his summer home; how he had moved southward with the icy winds and snows at his back, to appear here, like an emissary from the north, in the Lord's Woods. To verify our fox and to leave as Dave rounded up by telephone a different group of boys to go and find the owl.

Then to stomp home, avoiding now in broad daylight the garden of the long-suffering neighbor, leaving the soaking boots in the vestibule and begging from Eliza a grudging but certain breakfast. But still mentally out in all that white, even with the steam and warmth and burning cheeks and the glorious smell of bacon hissing.

# ELEVEN

# Spring

IT WAS MID-APRIL, but the woods were cold and windy. Crows brayed as we passed the Range, then flapped off one at a time toward the salt marsh. Down in the grass halfway down the Range a Killdeer called, took wing on the wind, and swept away, protesting. The woods were vaguely green now, the red maples beginning to blush their first foaming pink. Under the trees the woods were having their spring flooding: last week had been a hodgepodge of rain and snow, and some of the red maples stood in pools of black water. But around the pools the skunk cabbage was growing rapidly; it was already ankle high.

The Cinder Road was dry, as always, since it was elevated above the floor of the woods by two feet or more, and the waterworks crew kept adding, at regular intervals, a new dressing of cinders. Much later we were to learn that they called it the Brick Road, because its foundation had been, long ago, crushed brick. But cinders only, dark and fine, were all that one could see. In fact, Ben always called it the Black Road.

The willows by the cattail marsh were golden that day: yellow-green, almost in full leaf, and filled with blackbirds, a screeching congregation of cowbirds, grackles, and redwings. The wind whipped the slender branches where they clung like sailors to the rigging in a storm, but it never stopped their clang-orous conversation. And of course the spring peepers were in full chorus.

I walked around to Three Bridges and flushed a Bittern, watch-ing as it drew its bright green legs in, circled overhead, and then skimmed the treetops, heading out into the salt marsh. I found a night heron sitting motionless in one of the tall oaks, and then walked up the grassy pipe line to the waterworks, finding one solitary Fox Sparrow where last week had been dozens. That was funny, this morning, I thought. Roy had come charging into our physics class, right in the middle of an experiment on fric-tion, and had shouted, "Mr. Harrower! There's a Turkey Vul-ture sailing over the school!" And Dave had in one breath commanded, "Class continue the experiment. Be right back. Jake, take charge," and had run for the door, Duke and I on his heels. Clattered down the steps, out through the main entrance, across the driveway, and onto the lawn, just in time to see the black shape soaring eastward towards the woods. Where else would a science teacher flee a physics experiment in mid-course, just to spot a bird flying overhead? It was a crazy school. I loved it.

Mourning Doves were moaning somewhere, and from back in the woods on all sides, it seemed, came the sneezes of the Phoebes. I turned and walked toward the scout clearing, hoping for a Hermit Thrush, or a little band of early warblers. Finding nothing, I turned along the path that ran down along the Deep Ditch towards Foster's Brook. Near the end, on the right-hand side, the woods were flooded; a junco, and then another one, twittered like the ringing of tiny bells, moving from one tree to another. And then I spotted, down low, moving in quick starts around the underbrush, a bright yellow bird, a warbler!

I found it in my glasses and knew instantly that it was new to me: a bright yellow head, tinged with olive, the same color but a shade darker on the neck and undersides, with pure slate-gray wings and back. The notes I wrote down in my notebook for that day mention "fairly good size, for the family," and again, "the bill fairly large for a warbler, straight and black, the eye black with no ring, and no streaks on the breast and head." Then came a dawning realization and that hot thrill of discovery: I ran down the entire list of warblers and only one was possible: Prothonotary! But none of us, or anyone we knew, had ever found one on Long Island, and this was such an early date (where were the other warblers I should be finding now—the Black-and-white, the Myrtle, the Pine, the Yellow Palm?). And then again, the book I had showed the Prothonotary a rich orange yellow (the golden swamp warbler, some call him) and this bird was more an olive yellow. Could it be a female? Could it be something else entirely? No, it couldn't, but someone else would have to see it too, or no one would believe me. I looked and listened to his song, given only at great intervals, but sweet and clear. Then ran back along the Cinder Road, across the school grounds, to Dave's house.

Bud was there, and Tommy and Ben, and breathlessly I asked to see a book.

"What have you got?" they demanded, knowing I had something unusual.

"Don't know yet. A warbler. First let me see the plates."

"What do you *think* it is?" Dave insisted.

"You won't believe it anyway. Where are the warblers in here anyway? Here they are. Give me a minute."

"They crowded around as I riffled the pages. I wanted to be sure. Then I found the picture, but it only showed a brilliant orange male. I leafed through the other warbler pictures, then came back to the Prothonotary.

"Is that what you got us all excited about, a *Prothonotary?*" yelped Ben, outraged. Bud, rotating one finger at his temple, tilted his head like a loon.

"I'm pretty sure. Wait, let me read the description." Page 200. I found it, ran down the description of all the plumages, and came to "*Adult female in breeding plumage:* Similar to adult male but duller in color, the yellow duller or paler, tinged olive and less extensive about the head."

# The Lord's Woods

"That's it! That's absolutely it!" A female Prothonotary. In the woods, near the Deep Ditch. I had it ten minutes ago, maybe fifteen. Let's go!"

"Aw, Bibs, come on. It was an early Yellow, or maybe a Blue-wing!"

But I was positive. "Down low in a swampy wood? Dammit, come on. I'll *show* it to you! Come on!"

Finally and reluctantly they came, grumbling about my ineptitude, my imagination, or my hoax, with me sitting silent in the back of Dave's little car, keeping my fingers crossed, praying that it would still be there and we would find it. To save time, Dave drove around to the Old Gray Road and parked there, and we walked in along Foster's Brook. And, after almost no searching, we found the little warbler, heard her before we saw her, spotted her again where I had left her, hopping from one divided maple trunk to another close to the pools of standing water, admired her through Dave's twenty-power binoculars. Followed her through the soaking woodland for a half hour or more, as I accepted apologies and congratulations.

Later in the afternoon I brought another group out to see this most exciting stranger, but she was gone. But by that time, and from that day onward, my credentials as a bird watcher were secure. And that night I noted happily in my journal, "Griscom (the authority) says there have been *no* females recorded from our region. And his earliest Prothonotary is April 27!" And slapped a big black exclamation mark across the page.

All week long the weather had been fair and bright, but with winds out of the north and west. Each morning started cool and crisp, almost frosty, in spite of its being May, but by midday in the sheltered places the sun was warm. The trees were leafing out on schedule, tulips and hyacinths stroked color across the gardens; only the birds were overdue. In the woods yesterday all the birds we had seen were those that had arrived a week earlier, and most of them were the woods' own summer tenants, now busily engaged in proclaiming the boundaries of their nesting territories in songs and border skirmishes. It didn't seem quite fair to go an entire week in early May without a single new arrival. This was the most precious month and the most fleeting. Every day should bring its own new discoveries.

Then on Friday night the wind shifted and toward morning a warm rain began to seep from a misty sky. When I sat up in bed I could see that there was no wind, but the golden horse weathervane of Hewlett's barn was now running from the southwest. In the brief moment that I sat there, pushing aside the blanket, I could hear, over the caroling of the robins, the faint *wee-see, wee-see* of a Black-and-white Warbler, and the up-the-scale glissando of a Prairie. Any time there were warblers singing around the house, there would be warblers everywhere! Today all the signs pointed to a wave. After a week of adverse winds, with no birds moving, it should be a swell one.

Ben was already standing under the oaks on Howard Avenue (it had the tallest trees in the Lord Estate) when I arrived, no more than ten minutes later. He was bareheaded, but wearing an old olive-drab raincoat and what seemed to be not much else besides his moccasins. "Hi," I said, letting my bicycle find its own way into the bushes.

"Gee, Bibs," he said with awe in his voice and without taking the binoculars from his eyes, "the place is lousy with birds." Their voices proclaimed their presence before I found the first one. They came from everywhere, from the lower crowns of the red maples, from the second growth of swamp willows and gray birches, and lower still, from the eye-level thickets of viburnum and spice bush. Their sounds enveloped and thrilled me; I stood at the center of an orchestra with a hundred flutes, piccolos, penny whistles, and kazoos. All merged into one wild, improvised, but harmonious chorale. But if you listened carefully, you could distinguish each individual voice, for each piped its own special tune, in its own tempo, at its own pitch. And all the singers soaking wet!

We threw our heads backwards to scan the crowns of the tallest oaks. The trees were simply festooned with birds. The pale sea-green leaves had opened during the week, and the big bunches of blossoms swarmed with insects. But the warblers were everywhere. Without the binoculars, you could see leaves trembling and little bird forms, dark against the mist, darting in a dozen places all at once, as if weaving patterns on the webbing of the foliage. But to identify them, you had to find each in the binoculars and bring it down to earth.

So you would listen for a song, or watch for some movement in a leaf cluster, and then quickly move the binoculars from nose level to eyes. To see, at arm's length then, a clump of leaves twitching, then a bird form appear for a split second as it flashed a few feet lower, then hear it sing, then see it move two feet sideways, then bury itself in a blossom, visible again for one instant, then sing, then climb around a twig, showing only a flirting tail, then hop along a branch, then sing, then flit a few inches to another clump of leaves, sing again, then dart on buzzing wings six feet higher in the tree, then sing, then disappear behind a blossom, show a head, pull at a blossom, then become inaudible, motionless, and suddenly invisible, but finally, a few seconds later, dart across the road to another oak. Each tree was like a club with an ever-changing membership; when two birds left, three would join. Each bird with its own individuality and personality, each pursuing its own singular destiny, and yet all joined by some intangible bond: of wings, of song, of spirit?

I wiped my binoculars dry on a shirttail and looked upward. There's a Myrtle, and that one, I can only see his wing, that's another one, and there behind that branch is a third. This one looks yellow on the undersides with streaks, what I can see of him, and it must be a Prairie (I thought I heard one up there), and near it on the horizontal limb, creeping outward and around is a Black-and-white, now singing, and now gone. Higher up there, near the top, a bird is shaking a blossom, and I can see a white breast and now a trembling tail and there it turns and, oh, the head is a shining golden green and the throat and neck jet black; what a beauty, my first Black-throated Green! And from that spot in the tree comes the quavering buzzy song that Ben calls "The Lullaby of Broadway," because he sings the first few notes.

And now three newcomers to the tree: another Myrtle, this

one a brilliant male, another Black-and-white, and the third, just
below it on the left—hey, wait a minute, what's this moving behind that large thickening of leaves? The arms ached from holding the heavy glasses high, the craning neck began to complain.
But hold it steady, and be patient, the bird must move. There
he is now, part of him. Ben, look where I'm looking, here on the
left, can't see the head yet but he's yellow below, there, now
there, now there he goes, it's a Nashville!

And while I followed him, a streak of black and bright ver-
milion flashed across my field of vision and was gone. Hey, I
think I saw a Redstart! Yeah, Ben said, there's one straight over
your head about ten feet up. I leaned back to watch him flutter
about, a black-and-orange butterfly so graceful, so immaculately
poised and balanced, with a beauty so incredible, so shining
black, so flaming red on wings and tail, so totally, precariously
alive it made me want to leap and shout. Surely the most beautiful of all the birds, until the next bright warbler danced across
my vision.

We moved along the wet road a few feet at a time, calling
out our discoveries to each other, not bothering with every
Myrtle or Black-and-white or Parula, but saying them to ourselves, making a mental tally of each fleeting identity as it regis-
tered on our senses by sight or sound. Redstart, Redstart, Myrtle,
Parula, Yellowthroat, Goldfinch, Myrtle; hey, Ben here's a Kinglet. I just saw his Ruby crown! In the next tree we added a
Yellow Warbler, and another Prairie, three more Parulas, and
some more Myrtles, and another Black-throated Green. And then
heard a song like that of the Yellow, but more rollicking and
aggressive (the Yellow has a dreamy, tentative, almost musing
kind of song, as if he's singing to himself) and we both shouted,
almost together, *Chestnut-sided!* Found him, not high in the oak
this time, but creeping around the crown of a white dogwood
just coming into flower.

He came around the tree pausing to sing, with an almost jazzy
rhythm, and we admired his golden pate, his black face markings, and the chestnut stripe down his sides. He came so close to
us and seemed so fearless, or preoccupied, that we put our bi-

noculars down slowly to our chests and looked him in the eye, watching him throw his head back when he sang. Those bright black eyes conceal so many secrets, so many mysteries!

Where was he yesterday? we wondered. Close by, in southern New Jersey perhaps, held up for a week by those strong north winds? Or Delaware, or Maryland yesterday, and a few days earlier the red hills of Virginia, or North Carolina, and perhaps three weeks ago in Florida. And was he, when he began this northward migration, in the company of this same band of birds; was there a hidden bond between the Chestnut-sided here, and the two Redstarts overhead, and the Prairie, and that Yellow, and the three male Myrtles? And did they move together through the woods by day, and then by night as they flew northward in the darkness, keep in contact with each other by those strange, unidentifiable *cheeps* and *sssipps* and half chirps that floated down after midnight on any spring morning of a wave? Where did this little Chestnut-sided, this ounce or two of pirouetting feathers spend the winter, did you know? I thought it might be in the tropics, like Panama or Costa Rica, and tried to imagine this same bird gleaning insects from a palm leaf. How tiny and defenseless he was, how marvelous, how filled with unanswerable questions, and how impossible that such a mite could find his way back to the woodland patch where he was hatched; not here, but on some hillside in Connecticut, or Maine, Ontario, or Quebec. And that we should encounter him on his way!

"How many birds can you see moving in these trees now?" I asked, and Ben looked down on the road and up at the tall oaks, with the tiny bird shapes in their orbits and their every-which-way darting. "I dunno, there must be ten or fifteen birds in every tree, easy. So we've got two hundred birds right on this block. Maybe more."

"It's the biggest wave I've ever seen, I know, and you know what I keep thinking. About the millions of people sleeping in their beds who are missing this, who are never in their whole lives going to ever see a Redstart or a Black-throated Green or even a goldfinch.

"Hell, Bibs, they don't even ever know there is such a thing!"

# Spring

"And they'd think you were crazy if you told them what they were missing."

Ben laughed. "Most people think we're nuts as it is."

"Aw, who cares. Doesn't bother me." But it did, a little.

Slowly we moved up the road, listening for the songs of the birds, finding the singers by their movements and the motions in the leaves. Here, in a treetop a Solitary Vireo was industriously picking apart an oak blossom. From another tree, but hidden in a mass of leaves, a bird was saying, *Seek!* but we could not find him. *Seek*, he kept saying, and we walked completely around the tree. Then suddenly I remembered from last summer and shouted, "Rose-breasted Grosbeak!" "Yeah," Ben agreed, "it sounds like one, but where the devil is he?" Then we were distracted by another Nashville, a Redstart, two Myrtles, and a Black-and-white (a pale female this time), and when we looked back he was gone, but from the topmost pinnacle of the next tree up the road, a male Rose-breasted Grosbeak sang his rich, rolling carol.

There were other birds singing now on all sides, and the slow rain was coming to a stop. The trees still dripped, and the binoculars were a nuisance of smear and fog; mists hung low in the dripping branches. But from the deep woods to our left came the song of a Wood Thrush (who had arrived last Tuesday) and the trill of a Swamp Sparrow, and from the tiny swamp hole with the Private Property, No Trespassing sign, relic of that auction, a bedlam of spring peepers, Redwings, and grackles. Behind all the tumult, somewhere like a sound that was not heard because it had no beginning or end, the Mourning Dove's moan, like the hollow note you could make blowing across the neck of a sarsaparilla bottle. Nearer at hand, a Catbird seemed to be following us along the road, keeping his distance, but drowning out half the other music. We shied a pebble at him and he flew down and away, protesting like a cat. And in that moment of silence, heard a new song up above. A warbler sure, but which one? Not any that we had identified this morning, we were sure. One remembered from last spring? Now, let me think—it was more fun to say the name from the song and then discover you were right. A slower chirruping and then a faster part that ended almost in a trill. A little like that Nashville, but not a Nashville by any means. "I know, I know!" I said, rushing to get the word from tip of tongue to air, but I was beaten by Ben, who said it shyly, with a grin, "Tennessee?"

"Yeah," I said. "Tennessee," a little of the pleasure gone, but still excited. "Good one!"

We searched for the singer and found first another Chestnut-sided, and then a Parula, and then two Myrtles, and then a Scarlet Tanager, sitting motionless, quite in the open on a dead limb, the startling burnished velvet creature like a blessing, like a gift, like nothing that could be alive and fly and sing. Then that vireo again, perhaps the same one as before, with the Tennessee still singing lustily somewhere at the top; then a rush of little birds across the road to another tree and then silence from the Tennessee. And not until much later in the day, down in the woods near the water-works, did we hear that same song and find the singer, sure enough, a Tennessee. Two of them in one day!

The rain stopped, and though the warblers were still moving through the trees, we had now seen almost all of them, and many of them more than once. So we fished our wet bikes from the bushes and sped through the puddles to the woods. On the way adding another warbler, a Louisiana Water Thrush, bobbing along the road at one of the washouts.

There, by the Range, where the first high white oaks tower, we found another wheeling, darting concourse of birds, and under the trees Dave and Duke and Bud.

"Hey, you're late!" they greeted us. "Where you been? We've got a whole lot of new stuff: orioles and Black-throated Green, Prairie, Parula, Redstart, Chestnut-sideds, and Myrtles by the millions!" And a Blue-winged!"

"Yeah, we had all that too, and a Tennessee. Except the Blue-winged. Where didja get that?" And as if in answer, came the inhale-exhale buzzing note, from the topmost twig of the oak. "There!" said Dave, smiling. There, we thought, as we found him in the glass. The golden bird that sang that first day as we lay at Three Bridges, filling us with joy and sorrow and awakening.

We stood together looking and listening, and then moved

slowly down the Cinder Road through the woods' heart. Here, where the woods were mostly red maples with their roots in muck and water, the wave of birds thinned. But as we walked and stopped and walked again, we were aware that we were being watched, and avoided, by the dark forms of thrushes, deep in the woods.

"Hey, here's a Veery!" (At least he should be a Veery when he turns around.) Yay, a Veery! And from both sides of the road, both near and far, the insistent crescendo of a host of unseen Ovenbirds.

Some of us split off and took the Grassy Road and now the groupings were rearranged. But Duke and I were lucky, for in a grassy glade we found a tree with three tanagers in it. While we watched, the sudden police whistle—*breeep, breeep!*—of the Crested Flycatcher swiveled us around, and there he was, on the stub of a naked branch, now motionless, now flinging himself recklessly outward and upward on the air, doing loops and figure eights in pursuit of midges and May flies but aways returning to his perch to sit, cock his head, and go *breeep, breeep!*

"Crested!" we yelled, and the other gang called "Thanks, we hear it!"

We moved slowly down the Grassy Road, all green now and the pipe line all but concealed; in places the curving top of the pipe was visible, now the whole pipe exposed where it crossed a ditch. Here and there along its length, and in little glades, were brightly painted pipe fittings and massive iron wheels, marking the locations of the wells. Some painted red, some yellow and red, some rusty brown.

Up ahead of us was the brightness at the end of the cathedral, like a gold rose window. Here, open to the sky, the pipeline path crossed the cattail marsh in a wide grassy swath. Just before we reached it, we added four new birds. A Fish Crow calling. A band of night herons drifting across the treetops, squawking and jetting whitewash. A tiny green bird in a grape tangle with a humpty-dumpty, herky-jerk song, much louder than it should have been. We found it the same moment Dave's voice came booming across from the Cinder Road, "You fellows got a White-eye?" "Right here," we answered, grateful not to have to admit our uncertainty. White-eyed Vireo, of course. Finally, at the edge of the open marsh, a Woodcock. "Woodcock!" we bawl in unison, as the bird exploded up and away, zigzagging around the cattail marsh, crying *scaip, scaip*, in a kind of gasp. I thought back to that first day of discovery with Carl, when I kicked up the Woodcock, there at the entrance to the woods, without knowing what he was.

The other gang had found a water thrush, which we could hear far off to the left, and then a hummingbird, sitting on a pussy willow by Stepping Stones, but we couldn't find it when we ran over to look. Together we added more: along Teal Stream between Three Bridges and the Stone Bridge, a Solitary Sandpiper; and out in the open beside the stream, a Chebec—a Least Flycatcher. Underneath the Stone Bridge, the pair of Phoebes with a nest. And overhead, streaking northward, precisely due north, far above us, two attenuated loons. One behind the other. Each calling. Giving us that wild, primitive laughter as they passed.

Now we gathered around Three Bridges to pause and reflect. Dave had a card with all the local birds listed; you could get them in pads from the Audubon Society. How many have we got, fellas? The guesses ranged from forty-five to sixty. Calling each quickly as he checked it off, Dave ran down the list, each of us prompting, adding the names of birds we had seen or heard. "Don't forget the Green Heron we had early," Bud said, "those two we had in the rain." We added our kinglet and the nuthatch we had almost forgotten in the excitement of the warbler wave. Duke's Hermit Thrush, flushed near the Indian Tree, was doubted, because it was so late for them, but we eagerly called out the everyday birds we passed over so quickly earlier: the woodpeckers, the blackbirds, the sparrows, the flying-over birds like gulls and Black Ducks and that Great Blue Heron. "Hey, you forgot the Broad-winged Hawk!"

"What Broad-wing?" Ben and I howled together. "You didn't say anything about a Broad-wing! Where!"

"Right near the Range and out over the salt marsh."

# Spring

"Damn, why didn't you tell us?"

"It was gone before you got there." That hurt. A Broad-winged Hawk, or any hawk, was special.

"Sixty-nine," announced Dave. "Hey, that's pretty good. An even seventy with Duke's Hermit. And it's not even ten o'clock!"

"Aw, Dave, I know a Hermit Thrush, don't I?"

The morning was growing brighter, the sky so radiant that now the trees cast fuzzy shadows. Soon the sun would break through, and it would be hot. Wisps of steamy vapor rose from the soaked ground and from the marsh, and birds were singing everywhere. Not as overwhelmingly as at daybreak, but insistently, on every side. Here, in the oaks above the Stone Bridge, in the willows along the Cinder Road, and in the sweet gums that shaded Three Bridges, the wave was in full surge again, with warblers darting and creeping and fluttering everywhere. Even more of them, it seemed, than along Howard Avenue earlier, perhaps because there were fewer big trees, but here too there were more birds in the lower levels of the foliage. Redstarts splashing color everywhere, and Myrtles, Parulas, Black-throated Greens and Prairies, Yellows, Yellowthroats, Chestnut-sideds. More Nashvilles, another Tennessee, this one visible and "Hey," I cried, "here's a . . . a . . . a" (pausing as the bird plunged into a leaf cluster, showing only its tail). "A what?" Dave growled. "A Cape May! Just saw his head. Up there. In that big sweet gum. Way up. On the right. Not quite at the top. There, that shaking leaf."

"Bibs is right! By God, a Cape May! Good stuff. That's another good one!"

Splendid Cape May, with his citrine back, his sulphur-yellow head and the brick-red cheek patches. *Dendroica tigrina*, the tiger warbler, from the strong black streaks on his yellow front; he paused now to sing—a buzzy song, not aggressive like the redstart. We watched him work and listened to him sing, followed him from tree to tree, lost him, and then heard him, or another Cape May, far off across the woods. Then we came back to all the other birds, counts now lost track of, for we are adding more of every bird we saw before. Moving now slowly, in a loose

111

group down the Grassy Road, past the thick stand of small birches and sweet gums Carl and I had named, long ago, the Warblers Saplings. Warblers Saplings. Now decked with birds like animated Christmas tree ornaments. We scattered out, some of us to comb the oaks beside the Pipe Yard, others filtering through B.A.B., the Thrush Woods, and the Honeysuckle Woods, where Bud found, and showed Dave, a Hermit Thush, and instantly conspired not to tell the vindicated Duke until much later.

Behind the waterworks we were joined by Finny (just up), Roy, and Howie. They had started at the Pipe Yard, where the oaks had been full of warblers too; seeing most of the same species we had seen, adding only one rarity—a Blue-gray Gnatcatcher. "Where!" we shouted. "Around the other side of the marsh pond, you know the one you pass on Teal Trail. Where the big dead tree is." So three of us went racing back, searched, listened, found a sapsucker, kicked up our Woodcock for the second time, and finally heard the tinhorn pipsqueak signature of the gnatcatcher, finding him low down in willows, a slim, pale gray, elegant little bird, minding his own business, singing to himself, neat and dapper.

We ran back, caught up with the others, and went out across the Old Gray Road. But even before we reached the road, we could hear the three songs we came for: the lovely, pure, ascending trill of the Field Sparrow; bubbly cadenza of the Song Sparrow; and plaintive song of the Vesper. Calling with them, two Meadowlarks, maybe three. And our Killdeer, kicking up a rumpus about a tractor that was yammering across the fields. Finally, by the first farmhouse, we found our Bluebirds, sitting on fence posts, as swallows of three kinds stitched the air. Far off across the farm fields towards the airfield, a Sparrow Hawk was hovering, and from the creek below the farm came the whinny of a marsh wren.

Walking back, with all these new birds in our heads, Ben and I popped into a tangle across the Old Gray Road, where Foster's Brook came down from the north. The path didn't go very far—fifty yards or so—and then it ran into a marshy, muddy place almost impassible with blackberry and grape. This spot was really

# Spring

the northern outpost of our woods: this barrier had always stopped our explorations to the north. But beyond, we knew, was a small woodland, and then farms. Now as we entered the cool darkness from the road, we heard the last phrase of a warbler song; a ringing song we hadn't yet heard that day. We waited. A Catbird scolded. A Wood Thrush sang, and then a water thrush. Then a Redstart, a Yellowthroat, and from somewhere nearby, a Mourning Dove. Then that song again, full-throated, clear, and now quite close. And right down near the ground.

We stood and waited, and it came again, a little to the right now, just behind that maple tree. Held our binocular focused and ready. Then gasped, as the tiny bird flew up to a low twig, sat and sang for us, haloed in a single shaft of sunlight in all that darkened wood. Bright gold all over, with a green back and a black hangman's hood, except for the eyes and cheeks—a Hooded Warbler! Better even than the Cape May, the Broad-winged, even the gnatcatcher! Ben bellowed, "Hooded! Hooded Warbler! Come slowly!" Before long the whole gang, almost the entire club had silently moved in around us, watching one mite of an actor in his spotlight, singing his invitation that didn't quite sound the way the books transcribed it: "Come to the woods or you won't see *me!*" Even if it were quite true.

Back on the Old Gray Road, the Hooded still calling to us, we tallied up the list again. Now it was eighty-one. Eighty-two with Duke's Hermit, grumbled Duke. The rest of us smiled.

"Hey, let's make a day of it. It's only eleven o'clock and we could get a hundred easy. It's sure to be the big day of the spring. Eighty-one, without any marsh birds, or shorebirds, or ocean birds, except loon!"

Dave spoke. "Why don't all you kids hop on your bikes and get over to my house and we'll have some breakfast as fast as Elizabeth can fry some eggs, and we'll jump in the car and get on over to Lido." A shout went up. "How many can make it this afternoon? Roy? Fin? Bud? Bibs?"

"I've got a darn dancing class at two."

"Ben?"

"Saxophone lesson at three."

# The Lord's Woods

"Duke?"

"Dentist, but not 'till four."

"Well," I said, "I've missed three dancing classes in a row, and maybe if I miss the one today they'll throw me out."

"Aw," said Ben, "the heck with the sax."

"Dukie, you can call your dentist from my house. Now, I'm not advising any of you to play hooky this afternoon, am I?"

"No, Dave, of course not."

So we dashed up the Cinder Road, retrieved our bicycles, raced each other back to Dave's house, sat around the big square dining-room table, stoking eggs and toast and butter and orange juice and milk and coffee to an excited tumult of argument and laughter. Left Mr. Harrower's good wife a litter of devastated dishes and a carpet well muddied, and shouted thanks as the screen door banged six times.

We pried ourselves out of Dave's little Chevrolet and walked, spread out in a ragged line, across the flats. The sky was blue and cloudless and a soft warm breeze came off the ocean. Behind us were tumbled dunes that had been pushed up by the winds, in places twenty feet high. They screened our view of the sea and beach, except at intervals where concrete roads and sidewalks, half buried in drifting sands, cut through the dunes from boulevard to beach. Though each road had a street sign, there were no houses. We couldn't see the ocean but we knew it stretched endlessly there beyond the dunes by the plunge and suck of the surf, the pause and plunge again, like thunder.

Ahead of us as we walked, the landscape expanded in an endless panorama. Mud flats spread unevenly, red and brown and ochre, like a painter's autumn palette, with here and there a rain pool reflecting blue sky, with clumps of high-tide bush not yet in leaf, or a ditch cut straight, or a tidal creek snaking through to the bay. On either side of us, and in patches along the creeks before us, the fresh green spikes of bulrushes had appeared (we called them by their rightful names now—phragmites), shooting up from the yellow ruins of last summer. In some drier patches, the fine, matted green of the salt marsh grass—spartina. Far off

# Spring

beyond these flats was a wide deepwater channel, and beyond it, the even wider expanse of the salt meadow islands, a great green sea shimmering in the sunlight. To the right of us, the flats were margined by a wall of phragmites, the edge of an expanse that extended eastward for miles, although we knew there were little creeks and mud flats hidden there. To our left—to westward—and on higher filled ground, were the groomed green fairways, white bunkers, and wind-whipped flags of the famous golf links.

Dave and his butterfly collectors had found this beachside paradise quite by accident one day while out collecting the cocoons of moths (cecropia and polyphemus) to hatch in cigar boxes, and already it had become a favored and fruitful hunting ground. Open to the sky, with a sea wind and a sulphury smell, it was the very antithesis of our woods, yet a part of them, like the other side of a coin. This was an extension of the outdoor world that centered in the Lord's Woods, but had arms and enclaves in all directions: ocean, bays, ponds, reservoirs, and other woodlands. The woods were still at the heart of our world, but our arms were lengthening. Roy already had his junior driving license, and so had Howie. Soon Bob would have his, and then some day, if I could get permission, even I. Already, in trips with Dave, some of us had ventured as far as Montauk and Cape May!

Before we scarcely left the boulevard and pushed our way down through the bayberry thickets that bordered it, we were caught up in a whirl of motion. Overhead, swallows were cutting slices from the sky, weaving and streaking, chattering as they flew, and even more excitedly when they alighted, soft as weightless puffs of down, on the telephone wires to rest, observe, chuckle, and converse. Midget personalities in tailcoats, or so it seemed: Barn Swallows, Tree Swallows, and now a tiny Bank Swallow, and another, and six more! Higher overhead, gulls were wheeling; we had had them this morning over the woods; indeed, there were always a few soaring over the village to remind us how close we lived to the sea. Most of these were the common Herring Gulls, but among them were smaller gulls with black heads and mocking cries—Laughing Gulls—and there was one

ponderous and oversized giant, a Black-backed, a marvel of graceful motion, slanting off to seaward.

We moved forward cautiously, because the flats in front of us
were crowded with birds, and we had to do our best to approach
them without causing them to fly. Scurrying little posses of them,
motionless clusters of them, flying pairs in twisting pursuit, birds
overhead, birds far out on the channel, birds almost at our feet.

"Let's take it easy, men. Slow and easy. Duke, stand still!"

That's the way I wanted it, too. So many treasures out there;
let them come slowly, one at a time, with time to savor and enjoy them, time to get to know each bird, each flock. All spread
out here in front of us with no foliage to conceal them; just like
a painting in a bird book.

As we walked, a sparrow or two flew off in front of us;
Songs mostly, but one was a Savannah! "There, Roy, down on
the sand in front of that tuft of spartina, that's him singing." A
Green Heron flushed from a ditch, leaving a white jet behind
him. And here, on the first narrow stage of mud, running the
rim of a rain pool, three shore birds. Identical in every detail; we
knew them instantly: by size, their greenish legs, the streaks on
throat and breast, they're Pectorals! We watched them run and
stop and probe and pause and run again, then mew quietly and
probe again with quick jabs of their bills. We moved slowly toward them, inch by inch, until Duke staggered for some Dukish
reason, and they leaped into flight as one, quacking at us, arcing
and veering together, to land a hundred yards away.

"Aw, Duke, damn it," we complained. "Dukie," Dave warned,
"behave yourself or go back to the car."

"I stepped in a hole," he said sheepishly, and promptly stepped
into another.

We moved slowly forward again, down across the widening
stage, here baked and reticulated, here smooth and slippery, here
covered with an inch of water, here stippled with stray blades of
spartina, our feet kicking up galaxies of tiny flies. Moved closer
to the teeming concourse of the shore birds. There were thousands of them here: a thousand anyway! Each rain pool was
holding its own convention, some of the delegates standing mo-

tionless, as if hypnotized, all headed in the same direction, some perched on a single leg asleep, with head turned back and tucked into a shoulder. Some ran, stopped, ran again on slender scissoring legs, some skittered and flew, in groups of every size from two to hundreds. And they chattered in a dozen different voices. How far had they come last night, on their way from Argentina? How many miles left to fly, before they reached the tundra?

Most of them were small. You could hold one easily in your hand, if you could catch him. Their coloring was all in the same range: shades of brown and gray above, flecked, mottled, or speckled, with white below, some with streakings on the chest, some with a stripe or two. But there were bigger birds here and some of these had glossy black undersides, and some were uniformly gray or brown. The bills were all different, long, short, straight, curved. The legs were different lengths. But obviously, all these varied specimens were relatives.

The littlest birds were the most active; they scurried. You just couldn't believe how fast those short pipestem legs could crisscross. It was nothing like a bobbing step; they moved in beeline dashes, like those dancers who can tiptoe swiftly across a stage and seem to be on rollers. Those in the nearest congregation were all "peep," the smallest of the sandpipers. Most of them seemed to be Semis. (Who could seriously call a creature that size a Semipalmated Sandpiper?) But in among them, when we looked more closely, we found a few that seemed now, in the bright sunlight, a little rustier in tone, with thinner bills and pale green legs that proved them Leasts, the smallest of the peep.

When you look at peep, Dave reminded us, look at each one individually, because there are some rarer ones that are only slightly different. One, skittering along in front of us with the Semis, is definitely distinct; and I think he might be a White-rumped, from his size. But you can't be certain, until he flies or calls, because you can't see his white rump or hear his weak little *sssip* until he flies. So we kept track of him as he circulated in the crowd, like detectives at a railway station, trying to keep the marked man from disappearing in the confusion.

"Here's a Western," said Bob, who had joined us at Dave's.

Another peep so much like a Semi sometimes you couldn't surely separate them. But with a longer, stouter bill. We all looked, and Dave put his seal of approval on the Western; a fine discovery, particularly in spring migration.

We moved in closer, and still closer, until the little birds were almost underfoot. Some scattered, running away across the mud, but the rest flew up, and with them, without a doubt, was our White-rumped, and another we had missed. Both saying *sssip* the way a good White-rumped should.

Now we were further across the mud flat, skating a little on the slippery surface, sinking ankle deep in other places, each step carrying with it a gluey extra cargo.

Ahead of us, another mixed gathering surrounded a rain pool. In this crowd, more of a variety of size and shape. The proletariat were still the peep. But stalking among them, some more aristocratic figures: long-nosed Dowitchers, standing hip deep in water, immersing their whole heads as they foraged, a squadron of comical dowagers, as Bud called them. Standing taller, but no bigger in bulk, like giraffes among the antelope, a scattering of Yellowlegs, the nervous, noisy ones, teetering back and forth like hiccupping drunks. Why did they teeter? We didn't know and Dave couldn't answer; there had to be a reason but it hardly seemed necessary, for in fact they could stand as motionless as any other bird, if they felt like it, as motionless as those nearby plovers. The plovers were sleek and fat, standing frozen in decorative friezes, then running in short rushes, then standing again to *queedle* softly, a springtime-autumn sound. Some were still in their pale winter dress, but most were in breeding plumage, with their shining black undersides and gray-flannel backs.

The smallest plover on the stage was the most abundant. Out here in the center of the mud flats, we found whole companies and battalions of Semipalmated Plovers, the little ones with the sandy coloring and the black ring around the neck. Huddled together like little humps of sand, some standing, some sleeping, some preening, but none feeding. All facing the same direction, southwest into the wind, like a host of tiny weathervanes. Who wanted that breeze blowing up your tail and into every feather?

# Spring

Now we heard our first cricket-buzzing song of the Sharp-tailed Sparrow, like a lovely melody played on a one-inch violin. We spotted a Marsh Hawk quartering over the phragmites to the east. Watched a line of cormorants far off across the salt marsh islands, flying low, in close formation, moving eastward. Then brought our eyes back to the flats out ahead of us, where Bud had spotted a big gray bird, bigger than any shore bird we had seen thus far, standing motionless, dwarfing the nearby dowitchers, making no sound. All gray, with no markings to distinguish him.

Dave looked, and shouted, "By golly, Buddy, what have we here?" Some of us thought we knew what it was, but were reluctant to venture the name; it was a bird we had never seen before. "Come on guys, speak up. Buddy, you found it, now what is it?"

"Wal, Dave," answered Bud, in his high-pitched, down-East nasal drawl, which he affected sometimes in a deprecating way, as if mocking his own opinion, "up whar ah come from, ah'd be right sartin that there critter were a Willet!" Having spoken the name that was in our minds, we all now chorused it. It was a Willet indeed, a bird new to my lifetime list, and now if he would only unfold his wings we would be positive. We crept closer, looking long at him, then clapped and waved and shouted, and up he went, swooping low over the marsh, his zebra-striped wings flashing, his call saying his name clearly as he wheeled.

So many Semis and Leasts and White-rumps and Dowitchers, and Semi Plovers and Yellowlegs and Black-bellies everywhere, and here was a little squad of new ones: Red-backs. Not far away, some paler sandpipers, but streaky, the same kind you saw playing tag with the surf all summer; these were Sanderlings busily feeding. Then overhead a squealing, squawking visitation of Least Terns, giving us the eye, warning us away, circling around us like a pack of beggar children except that they were graceful and snowy, with swallow wings and yellow bills snapping the blue sky. Now we roused two Black Ducks up from the deepest creek, and then two more and two more, and the six went down the channel low and fast, with much complaining.

# The Lord's Woods

We stopped to admire two Knot, the beautiful pink "sunrise" birds, I always thought them, with a grace and gentleness and an air of substance about them, unlike the common, scurrying peep. Lastly, just before we reached the channel, we discovered a single turnstone, the crazy mottled harlequin of shore birds, balancing on one red leg.

We stood on the sandy shore, kicking the mud from our shoes, surveying the channel and the salt marsh islands, and heard behind us, in the spartina, the spluttering buzz of the Seaside Sparrow that in his ears, or at least his mate's, was music. We chased the dark little sparrow from bush to bush, and quickly got back our burdens of mud. Then swung around as Fin yelled, "Bittern!" to see the light brown heron gliding across the marsh away from us. How had we missed him out there? Easy, the way they stood and stretched and froze among the phragmites.

Now I found a pair of Red-breasted Mergansers, in fine spring plumage, swimming across the channel, and a remnant flock of wintering scaup hugging the far shore. And turning, pleased at these unexpected discoveries, hollered, "Hawk, a falcon, a *Peregrine!*" as the slim shape came streaking out of the west, over the golf course, down across the mud flat, making a pass at the dowager club and scattering them like chaff before him, but not pausing to take one, soaring upward again on curving wings, flying hard eastward to disappear—all in ten seconds. Did you see the black mustache? He was a dark one, big, too. Probably a female, from the size. Those shore birds really panicked. One beautiful Peregrine, one beautiful and doomed Peregrine, speed king of the skies, on his way home to Maine or Quebec, Labrador or even Greenland. In a hurry! How many pairs of eyes would see him on his way?

Now we turn back toward the car, this time skirting the drier edge of the mud flat, where the birds were less abundant: here the lonely individualists who for reasons of their own avoided the tumultuous concourse around the rain pools. Here we found a few more Pectorals, and added a Spotted Sandpiper and two Piping Plovers, as Marsh Wrens blurted their phrases of nuptial hysteria from the phragmites. Back at the car we took another count. Not yet three o'clock, and the list had reached 106 species!

Fifteen minutes later we were racing barefoot through the tumbled dunes at Point Lookout, eastward from the village, running the grassy paths in hidden valleys, scrambling up the sliding slopes to reach a summit, to stand and scan and leap the other side. The white sands were dazzling now, each grain gleaming like a diamond; even the stiletto blades of beach grass glistened with sun sparks. The valleys between dunes were hot and airless, clouded with mosquitoes, endless. But finally, a half mile from the car, we emerged from this wind-carved tumble of birdless hills, panting and triumphant at the water's edge, on the smooth hard sand of the Inlet.

First we looked out across the surging waters, where milling gulls and screaming terns circled and chased; then across to the far shore, where gulls and more shore birds stood in silent ranks; then swept the waters of the inlet and the ocean with our binoculars, finding a few late-lingering ducks and a grebe or two, almost invisible against the opposite shore. Finding it a challenge and an enigma each time a band of shore birds, racing across the inlet, veered and weaved in unison, with an alternation of sudden light and dark, each individual precisely the same distance from his neighbors but never touching, each bird mirroring the twisting path of every other. But how? Do birds, like fish, like some flocking animals, communicate in ways unknown to man, and if so, how sensitive must this communication be, to permit this split-second coordination!

Dave had found, out across the bay almost a mile away, standing on a sand bar and undulating in the heat waves, what seemed to be a white heron. From its size, surely an American Egret—a rare bird indeed—and worth that hot run through the dunes. Six new species were added here, in addition to the turnstones, sanderlings, and peep at our feet; remember them when we total the abundance of each species.

An hour later we stood at the edge of another world: a prairie.

# The Lord's Woods

Here on the Hempstead Plains is the only true prairie, Dave said, with typical prairie flowers and grasses, to be found anywhere east of Indiana. Flat, uncultivated, these fields stretched in all directions to the horizon, a horizon punctuated here and there by a farmhouse, a line of telephone poles, or a fence. Beneath our feet was a wild green carpet of unmowed grass, and hidden in their depths, a tapestry of wild flowers: the pale blue of Bird's-Foot Violet, Blue-eyed Grass, and Yellow Star grass, the pink of Polygala, the yellow-pink of Salsify, the yellow-orange of Sundrops, and over all the yellow haze of Canada Hawkweed. But today was for birds, and somewhere out there, standing motionless in the grass were Upland Plover. If we spread out and walked slowly across the fields we might find one. And once again our luck held out: we heard the liquid calling of the bird beyond the first fence, saw it fly to a fence post, watched the graceful, soft-speckled form of the bird as it posed against the sky, then found three more as we searched, discovered in a wetter meadow with taller grass, a colony of Bobolinks, most beautiful of all our blackbirds, and most musical.

Now we wound down the lanes that lead to the North Shore, stopping here to search in an orchard for an Orchard Oriole, there to listen for a Bob White in a meadow, again to watch a Bluebird enter a hole in a fence post and remember this fence for future observation, now to invade, stealthily, or at least unobtrusively, a pine grove on a large estate where Duke insisted he heard a Pine Warbler. Which turned out to be, not as we had predicted, a Chipping Sparrow, but a Pine Warbler. Finally, to the lovely valley of Mill Neck, with its carefully manicured estates sloping down to tidal marsh and estuary, to the fresh-water lake above the dam, to the marshy woodland above the lake, with its giant tulip trees. And here again we encountered the flood of migrating warblers; in the trees, on the hillsides, in the underbrush along the stream. Less active now in the shadows of later afternoon and far less vocal, but everywhere around us. We found more of almost all those birds we had seen that morning in our woods, adding only a Magnolia in a dogwood, and one snarling Black-throated Blue. But here at Mill Neck we found two hawk's nests, one a Red-shoulder's and one a Broad-wing's, watched an Osprey cruising over the salt marsh, discovered a pair of Wood Ducks swimming in the stream above the railway trestle, and from that trestle added all the other swallows we had missed earlier, a Pied-billed Grebe, and last—oh, marvelous discovery—a Least Bittern in the cattails!

The light was waning now, holding darkness in the valleys in spreading pools, turning all the leaves from pale green to dark, silencing the birds; the migrants now were asleep in little invisible groups, fattened up again after the long day's feeding, and ready for another lap of their journey that would begin some time after midnight.

The long day that had begun in the mist and rain with Ben on Howard Avenue seemed to have stretched on for endless hours. During the long drive home we argued whether to count the Henslow's Sparrow we almost surely heard there in the Bobolink field, but never saw, or Duke's Hermit Thrush (we let him argue with increasing outrage for a while, and then admitted we'd seen another), and whether we had seen both Greater and Lesser Yellowlegs, or only Greater. Finally, with Dave acting as referee and arbitrator, we arrived at our approved total, added once by Roy and checked by Bob: 138! More birds than we had seen during the entire first year that we had been keeping any records.

Dave drove us to his house, and we rode our bicycles in darkness to our various homes, faces burning with wind and sun, mud caked on shoes and ankles, legs crisscrossed with catbrier slashes. Dinner had been kept hot; there had been some anxiety but at five o'clock Mrs. Harrower had reported that we were making a day of it. I'd been dropped by Madame Rousseau's School of Modern Dancing, which was cause for a lecture but probably just as well; there were only two sessions left and no sign yet of any aptitude. Then I wolfed the steaming pot roast, rice and gravy, and a big, mouth-melting wedge of Eliza's magnificent orange layer cake. With the words pouring out and the books all spread across the dining room table to show with joy and pride the exciting birds we'd seen.

There it should have ended, with the list at 138, with a thou-

sand images crowding the mind, and the glow of the most splendid of all the days in memory. I knew then that no matter how
long I lived, this first great overwhelming day of spring migration would live with me, that I would always recall, as I did with
each new bird I ever saw, just how the weather was, and the
light, and the time of day, and who was with me: the Willet on
Lido marsh, the Hooded Warbler on the Old Gray Road, the
Upland Plover on the prairie fence post, the Least Bittern creeping through the reeds at Mill Neck, and the sweet, wind-wavering
calls of Bluebirds across the fields at Locust Valley.

But the day was not quite over. In the garden after dinner the
air was still warm, a three-quarter moon was coming up over
Carl's house, and from the distant woods I could hear the chorus
of the peepers. My parents had gone to their party, Richard was
at the movies, Johnny, who was seven, was supposed to be in
bed, sent there early after an episode of stomping around in a
deep puddle with shoes and socks on, before an admiring ring
of little girls. I could tumble into bed myself and be asleep in
ten seconds, or I could go back to the woods and listen for that
Woodcock; in another half hour the cattail marsh would be
flooded with moonlight.

So I picked up the bike again and stopped around for Bob and
Ben, whose parents had decided that their birding for the day
was absolutely over, then found that Bud was home and willing.
We rode to the entrance of the Cinder Road, left our bikes, and
walked into the woods. No sound now from the birds sleeping
all around us; only the crescendo of the peepers—all of an inch
long and audible one mile away—singing harmony for the occasional bellow of an early tree frog. We walked together down
the black tunnel of the Cinder Road, with no light anywhere
but the moon, reached the Stone Bridge, and turned up Teal
Stream to Three Bridges. Here we stopped and listened, dangl-
ing our legs over the dark water with the moon riding in it.
All the pale spring greens of the leaves had now turned to silver; black shadows streaked across the marsh in front of us,
the trunks of the taller oaks. A hazy mist hung over the marsh;
in the moonlight it seemed to have an inner glow, blue and ethe-

real. All around us, like an enclosing wall, the dark and silent mystery of the woods.

But the peepers in the marsh were loud, their calling coming in cycles, now growing in volume and voices to a shrill screaming, then fading until only few were giving voice, or just one, or none. Then, after a silence, the same one began again, hopefully, questioning his group, asking for some sort of amphibian confirmation. The answer came from some dark pool nearby, and then a neighbor put in his two cents worth, and then a few other eavesdroppers had something to say, and then the entire lunatic asylum was yelling at once, full cry.

If the woodcock is here, I thought, we'll never hear it over this commotion. Neither of us have ever heard a woodcock's flight song; all we knew was that scraping call when we kicked one up from a thicket. But we knew what to listen for: first, that loud nasal *bleent* from the ground, and then when the bird took wing for his dance, a long musical twittering, a louder chirping, and then silence. Then from the ground again, another *bleent*. That's what the books said, anyway. Was it true that when a woodcock returns to earth from his dance, he lands precisely at the same spot he left? Was it true, as we had heard, that if you run to the spot where the first *bleent* sounds, and lie down on your back, keeping motionless, the woodcock will sail in and land on your chest? If we hear one tonight should we try it? Sure, great, swell—if the woodcock doesn't cry from the marsh!

The moon rose higher now, its upper rim just clearing the tops of the maples to the south, the marsh between us still in light and shadow. We waited, listening, shivering as much from the growing chill in the air as from anticipation.

And then, with the moon full up above the trees, with a misty halo around it, and the light beginning to creep across the marsh away from us, we heard it! *Bleent! Bleent!* again. Loud and nearby, straight down the center of the pipe line. We held our breaths, or so it seemed, and waited. *Bleent!* And then a long pause, of several minutes, and the *Bleent!* again. Now the tempo seemed to have quickened. *Bleent!* And faster, *Bleent, bleent!* Were all the calls coming from the same spot? We could not be sure; we could see nothing; it sounded as though the bird were walking around between each call. Now, with no more than a three-second interval, a series of calls, above the peepers clamoring, and then silence.

Now, miraculously, the peepers themselves were silent. And suddenly, from high overhead, up somewhere with the blue stars and the irridescent moon-blue air, we heard the song beginning. A silvery, gossamer twittering that seemed to be floating down from unseen flights of angels, a scattering of notes like milkweed seeds on the wind, that climbed up and up the stairs of night, the notes themselves growing higher and more tinkling, as if the singer was swinging in wide circles above us, ever higher, ever farther away. We stood with our heads thrown back, our mouths open, and our eyes straining, but nothing could we see: no spiraling black shape, no moonlit shadow, and no angel.

The twittering was reaching a climax, high up there over us, halfway to the moon. Suddenly the silver necklace was broken, the bird was still climbing, still moving higher, but breathlessly singing now in short phrases, as if the little singer was gasping for air, and for heart, in one last ecstasy of music. Then, for one brief minute there was silence in the sky; the singer had dissolved into thin air, or entered into heaven. But no, there was a new song now, a series of blurted notes, wild, drunken, uncontrolled, growing louder with each moment. Now the woodcock was on his downward sleigh ride, coming down the moonbeams not in a spiral glide, but in a series of zigzag, rocking dives. Louder and wilder—almost hysterical—came the blurted phrases, as if the bird could not quite control his singing or his descent, until it seemed that the singer was just above the trees. Then once more, no sound except the peepers, beginning a new quorum. And now, from almost at our feet, a *bleent!*

He sang and danced for us that night a dozen times, and climbed and spun around his circular staircase twittering, gasping, almost dying, then diving on his invisible trapeze. And each time we heard a new song beginning in the sky above us, we'd madly dash across the grass to the exact spot where we'd heard the last call. Fling ourselves down, taut and rigid on our backs, listening for the climax, and then the diving return, and then the silence; not even daring to breathe now, bracing for the little bird to land on chest or belly. Then it would come, *bleent!* from a few yards away. Mocking us, and our sodden sweaters. Now we know it: woodcocks do not return to the same spot each time, at least not this one, with the two of us here, so plainly visible in the moonlight to his keen eyes. But once, just once, we were rewarded with a quick shadow, in the mist and the moonlight, of the dark bird shape an instant before landing. How swiftly he dove through the darkness!

Now he left us, moving far off across the Cinder Road, bleenting at long intervals, but no longer singing. We were cold and wet with dew. So we walked back slowly to our bicycles, marveling at our day and our world, and at the unseen singer in the moonlit air.

# TWELVE

# Summer

I HAD BEEN SAYING her name for almost a year before I met her. She was the loveliest little human being I had ever seen, and the first time she passed me on Broadway in the village and set off sparklers in my skull I was with Chee, who knew the names of almost all the girls our age in town, or knew someone who could find out. He said that she had recently come to town from Virginia with her little brother, and that they lived with their aunt on Centre Street. She was sixteen and her name was Anne. She was so beautiful she stopped my heart and made my whole world suddenly luminous.

After that first encounter I saw her now and then having sodas with a giggle of girls around a table in the back room of the Colonial Pharmacy, seeing only her in the crowd as if all the rest were faceless, or walking with her brother in hand on some errand along Broadway. Once it was in the post office; she was alone and smiled at me, flooding me with sudden joy and panic, and once down near the bay we passed in walking and we both said, *Hi!* and I was filled with an agony of shyness, wanting to stop her, take her arm, and tell her how these glimpses of her (and just the knowledge that she existed) graced my life. But I was tongue-tied, and we passed without pausing and then I turned to watch her slender figure receding down the road and found her looking back at me. We laughed at that.

I saw her at football games that autumn, her pale hair shining around her shoulders over a yellow slicker. I loved the way she tossed her head to make her hair fly; I loved the gentle modulated way she spoke and the smile she always gave me with a dip of her head and a lowering of her wide green eyes, as if we had an understanding or a little secret shared against the world. I began to look for her whenever I walked in the village, and sometimes strolled down Centre Street to the Cherry Desert just in the hope of seeing her, but even those encounters, dizzy and delicious, came infrequently. Even then, I could only blurt "Hi Anne!" like a blithering dumbstruck fool, which I was. So often when I saw her, some oaf or other was with her leaning his shoulder against her or crowding her in ways that seemed embarrassing to her and an outrage to me.

Then one evening the following June there was a party and she was there. It was another of the usual Saturday evening school groups at somebody's house, with the boys horsing around in one room and the girls chattering in another and some dancing to a phonograph and a lot of noisy silliness and some showoff, puerile dirty talk and a cluster of boys and one girl (Claire, of course) ostentatiously smoking cigarettes, and later with couples paired and sprawled around the furniture and the floor and most of the lights out. Anne was dancing with Joe, and then Butch and Rog and Andy, I was sitting against a wall talking birds with Roddy, but not taking my eyes from her, watching as one after another of them tried to persuade her to stop dancing and go out on the lawn or anywhere, watching as she whirled laughing to the music like an enchanted leaf in the wind. So lovely. So unspoiled. So impossibly perfect. Once or twice our eyes met and over a shoulder she gave me that secret smile that knifed through me and made me sick with longing. Then someone kicked over the Victrola and there was no more "Hit-of-the-Week" music to dance to.

Suddenly there was a honey-soft voice whispering "Hi, Robert" in my ear, and I turned from Roddy and it was she, on one knee at my side, her hand held out to me to help her sit beside me, the other hand with half a cookie to pop into my open mouth.

So then at last the talk came, but what we said I cannot tell, because I was overwhelmed by her nearness, my thoughts in wild disarray, my tongue answering not to my mind but to my excitement, because she was here, the beautiful dream, sitting facing me on the hassock, so close that our knees were touching, her hair a silkfall down her shoulders, her little heart-shaped face with its big green eyes turned up to me, so intent, so innocent, so wise, so dear. Not even hearing half her questions because my chest was pounding and inside I was feeling, "Keep this, oh, keep this, please let no one try to end this." Then slowly the confusion ebbed and I was myself again, talking comfortably, disarmed by her gentle manner, her interest in me, and her little understanding laugh. Two or three boys came over and tried to pull her away, but she disengaged herself sweetly but with finality. How much more poised she is than I am, even though a full year younger! Gradually the crowded room, the babble of voices, even the squeals of laughter—the entire world around us—receded and then vanished and we were alone, our faces close together, a few silky strands of her hair brushing my cheek, and looking into each others eyes, murmuring like two lovers who had always known we would find each other.

Later I walked her home through a darkened village to Centre Street, leaving the party with her much to the utter disbelief of Joe and Chee and Butch and some ill-disguised envy on the part of Andy and all those self-confident extroverts whose lives revolved around the pursuit of girls. Her aunt was waiting at the door and we said good night primly and properly and with a handshake, and I walked away feeling foolish again, inadequate and immature, all of which I was, but floated home two feet above the pavement.

The first time I took her out for an evening she looked young and fragile and smelled so sweet, just like a baby, with a kind of

131

delicate milky fragrance, and I wanted to touch her and take her in my arms. She sat up straight on her side of the seat of my father's car with a big bow under her chin, with that ashen hair falling down around her bare shoulders, and I thought she was beautiful beyond believing, even in the darkness, the half-light smoothing her cheeks and her chin, the lashes and the eyes in shadow, and she looked like an angel. But we were strangers all over again and she was quiet, both of us aware that this was our first date, our first time alone together. At the movie she sat straight-backed and prim although our shoulders were touching.

Once I stretched my arm around the back of her seat, but she made no effort to lean back or touch it, and after a time my fingers started to tingle and grow numb and I withdrew my arm. Once accidently I brushed her fingertips with mine and she pretended not to notice. We were both sensitive to each other's every breath, unsure of how to break down the barriers of our shyness, knowing only that we must. Then I found my courage, reached for and held her fingers in my hand, and they were warm and slender and small and curled inside of mine. But the old Columbia Playhouse that summer night was steamy hot and our hands got wet and finally we pulled them apart to applaud an atrocious vaudville act, two inept juggler-comedians dying in front of that old painted street scene with all the local store signs on it—Columbia Garage, Teddy's Restaurant, Nebenzahl's Dry Goods Store, and the Cornega Meat Market (strictly kosher).

In the car after the show she still sat up straight like a prim little Puritan child at church. But smiling in the darkness, and not as far from my side.

We drove around aimlessly, down towards the beach and then back between the two golf courses and then (praying that she would refuse) I asked her whether she would like to stop at Yarlie's for something—a milk shake or to dance. She said she thought she would like to drive a little to cool off, so we didn't stop anywhere. I wanted to be alone with her and not share her presence with anyone. In the darkness she looked tremulous yet trusting, eager but unsure.

# Summer

We drove through the park and down to the bay to the old open wharf where the fishermen and the oystermen and the rumrunners brought in their boatloads, but there were the black forms of other cars parked there, so I turned and went up the road past the booth where, some said, our policemen collected their dues from the big, dark, canvas-covered trucks that rumbled mysteriously up from the wharf at night, and I could see that she was smiling in the darkness and then I could feel her knee almost imperceptibly move against mine, perhaps unintentionally but not quickly withdrawn. I wanted to hold her in the circle of my arms and press her close to me, baby smell of her neck and cleanness of her hair, and kiss her heart-shaped little face in fifteen places. And now my leg was against hers and she could tell that it was there deliberately and that I knew she knew it, but she just sat up straight and smiling, close to me.

I went past our house to show it to her, but all was darkness except the big ship's lantern over the door, left lighted for me, and then drove, or perhaps the car found its own way somehow, toward the woods, excitement mounting in me. Once, as we entered the blackness of the woods, and I dimmed the lights past Quinn's farmhouse, she looked at me questioningly, without speaking, and we went around the S-curve of the Cinder Road and reached the Range, where the pipe barrier still blocked the road. I turned off the road and stopped under the giant white oak where the Rose-breasted Grosbeaks were nesting, where John had found the rare Whorled Pogonia growing, turned off the lights and the ignition. Here we were at last, in my woods— in my home—in my beloved world, the two of us together! The throbbing sounds of the summer night surged in through the open windows: the tree frog chorus, the insects screaming as they always did, like people who had one day left on earth and wanted to be counted. The air moved in hot and wet and rank with greenery and summer, and a few fireflies semaphored.

She was closer to me now, young and warm and sweet, and we were in darkness, her faced turned to me. My hand went to her shoulder and I moved her gently with no pressure, just a touch, and she responded, moving slightly, and I could feel her hair under my hand and my fingers tightened and I leaned forward and kissed her, high on the cheek. And then kissed one eye that closed under my lips, and then the other, and then an ear, and then her neck below the ear, and then her throat that was lifted slowly to me, and then her chin as her face came down to me, and then her mouth, first a teasing brush as she moved away, then the faintest touch, motionless. Then she moved in to me and pressed her mouth, half open, against mine. And I could feel her knee against my thigh, as she turned to me. How small she was, inside my arms!

We kissed and clung together; I kissed her hair and forehead and ears and throat and she kissed me in light flickerings of her lips, and then our mouths would find each other and were locked in a hunger until we lost our breath, and the blood was pumping loudly through my ears, all the nerves in my legs and thighs and in the pit of my stomach were humming like a crescendo of bees, and all the words I wanted to say, the cherishing words, the wondering words, the words of this new excitement and this fever and this revelation of love and longing were locked inside me. Then we broke apart and she leaned back away from me, against the car door, and looked up at me, smiling her secret smile, and whispered, "Boy!" and I sighed, "Anne!"

She arched her back in a slow, delicious stretch, the backs of her hands lifting her hair from her neck, her elbows moving outward and upward, her head stretching upward and away, her little round breasts high now, so gracefully, so innocently sensuous. I moved my cheek to her breast, to the warmth and girl fragrance and the slow insistence of the beating heart, and she held my head against her.

"A woman in a black cape."

"What's that?"

"That big tree over us. The branches against the sky. Like a mother with her child, spreading her cloak around her baby. Can you see?"

I lifted my head and looked upward through the open window behind her head. Yes, the sheltering arms of the tree spread like a mother's arms over her children. I buried my head again. It was beautiful, and vaguely disturbing. The mourning cloak.

She stirred.

"Do you want me to move?"

"No. I have a present for you. An olive branch." I moved and took her leafy offering.

"That's sassafras," I said. "It has a taste I like." I split the twig down the middle, and we each chewed, the taste bitter and aromatic after the soft kisses. Suddenly, overhead, the furious rasping of an early katydid, and she imitated him, "Katy-did-did-did! Katy-did-did-did-did!" And we laughed.

I took her in my arms now, feeling the warmth coming from her sweetly, the secret smile now inches from my face. And put both hands under her chin and lifted her little face and kissed her, framed in my fingers, and she leaned forward, kissing me now gently, now eagerly, her mouth half open, the tip of her tongue flickering between my lips, making me gasp each time she did it. Her whole being was here within the arc of my sensitivity, so soft, so small, so perfect, so vulnerable. My arm moved, my hand under her chin dropped, across her throat and her collar-bone, and suddenly, without conscious recognition and then with a sudden realization that brought a tempest of bees to my thighs, my fingers were around the swell of her breast. I moved them over the smooth fabric lightly, cupping the woman of her —the round, soft, resisting, movable miracle, sensing the impudent button centered there through her dress.

She stirred slightly at my touch, as if to break away, but held her mouth to mine; now we were breathing hard and the harp strings in my loins were screaming, flooding me with an infinite hunger, a delight, and a sense of wondering gratitude. Finally we snapped our heads back breathless and she gasped and whispered, "Oh, Robert," not in reproach but in discovery, and I answered, "Anne, darling." We moved away from each other now, recognizing danger, looking into each other's eyes, a year of longing for me now resolving in felicity beyond all dreaming. Out across the Range, fireflies were winking.

"Take me in your arms," she purred, and curled up like a

kitten to lie in my lap, her head in the cradle of my left arm, up against my chest, her legs curled beside me on the seat.

"Oh, Robert, I waited a whole year for you to ask me for a date. I thought you never would. Why did you take so long?"

"I was afraid to. I guess I've always been afraid of girls, but especially you; you filled me with panic. You know I always seemed to act like an absolute idiot around you."

"Oh, I didn't think so. Just very quiet."

"It was pride too, I guess. I was sure you would turn me down, and that would have shattered me. You always had a pack of boys around you. I'm such a dunce with girls."

"The truth is—I hate those boys," she whispered, kissing me lightly. "All of them. They're so darned clever. All of them out after something just for themselves. So sure of themselves, and all with just one big idea. To them, I'm some kind of a contest: who will win the big kewpie doll, who will be the first to get Anne Martin. They've all got a fast line and it's just selfish, thinking of themselves." She lifted her face and kissed me.

"I don't think I have a line," I said. "I don't have any idea what boys say to girls—when they're alone together. All the girls I've grown up with at school are more like sisters. We've been together in the same classrooms since we were five, we've all known each other and our families ever since we got out of diapers and I've had a different favorite every year. But never one of them enough to make a fool of myself for her. I guess I never could overcome the feeling that anything personal or intimate I might say to a girl would sound trite and silly and obvious, and that she would laugh at me. Oh, heck, I can't explain it. I suppose I should admit that I never grew up when it came to girls. With you, for the first time, I . . ."

"Say something to me, Robert. Say something trite and silly and obvious." I knew what I could say. I had said it to myself over and over.

"I love you, Anne. Your beauty caresses my soul."

She kissed me savagely then and moved closer into my embrace, flicking her tongue between my lips and my senses swam and my arms came up to hold her tightly to me, our mouths locked together, our bodies straining, now one, a unity, a fusion and a miracle, the world contracting into a tiny sphere enclosing only us, the two of us here in each other's arms. Her wide eyes with its fringing lashes closed as we kissed, the sweet, baby, milky scent at her throat, the cool sleekness of her bare shoulder, her breathing that came swift now; all our senses consumed in this moment of awakening. And now my right hand rested on one knee and now on the incredible softness inside her leg above it, and she stirred and murmured a little protest, but her grip on me tightened and she pressed her legs together to clasp my hand between them and I was glad because I wanted her desperately to want me to go no further and to help me stop, and now we kissed feverishly, mouth, eyes, ears, throat, shoulder, neck, and mouth again, both breathless, hearts pounding, our senses in riot, and then her legs locked and held my hand, and she arched against me quaking with a little moan, buried her face in my chest, and then was still. And then half sobbed, half shivered, still in my arms, warm and small and tender, tears running down her cheeks and mine. "Oh, Robert, I never . . . no one ever . . ."

Suddenly the world outside came flooding in on us: the insistent buzzing of the katydid, the doomsday keening of the insects, the endless trilling of the frogs, the rank fragrance of the green-gone-black world of summer, the fireflies sending their random signals to anyone who would read them: "Look! I'm alive! I'm alive!" And over us the Lord's Woods spread their mantle like a blessing.

And it came to me that these two, the girl I had found and the woods I loved, were joined together deep inside me, in some remote center of my being that I could sense and feel and that could make me long and ache, but that I could never wholly understand. Was it because they were both symbols of something fresh and unspoiled and virginal and lovely, and therefore precious beyond imagining? Was it because they were both mysteries, both sources of unending surprises and delights, secrets to be discovered, blessings to be savored? All I knew was an overpowering joy and an awareness that right now, right at this moment, at this time of my youth, at the heart of this flowering of our love, was an aching, fleeting instant to be captured and held forever. That if I lived for another century there would be no more poignant time for me; that the unspoiled woods and the unspoiled girl would together be the story of my youth. That when you are eighteen and in love the world could never be as fresh and clean and beautiful as this again, nor so filled with promise; that this was the springtime of our lives that comes once to each of us and never comes again.

We drove home slowly, her head on my shoulder, and I let the car go at a crawl, wanting the spell never to break, wanting never to let her go, but she said drive fast! and I let the night streak past and the white road fly under us, and then we kissed once more at her house, a gentle good-night, God-bless-you kiss, and with a motion of flying hair she was gone.

We came back to the Range on other whispering nights that summer and put the world away from us. Other evenings, but only if we had it to ourselves, we stopped the car on the ancient wharf where the village meets the bay. Paused for a moment with headlights stark against the oyster sheds, the piles of oyster shells, the white rowboats and workboats hanging out on the black water, and far across the channel the squatters' shacks, on piles above the salt marsh. Then all was sudden blackness, with the lap and hiss of wavelets against the rotting bulkhead, the painters of the rowboats flapping and creaking in the darkness, now and then the cry of heron or shorebird on the air, or chatter of rail from the marsh. And in the curve of my arm the precious head, the sweet scent of her throat, the quick heartbeat under the blouse.

But it was Anne's Tree at the Range in the Lord's Woods that more often drew us and spread its arms in benison over us, as we clung together and murmured secret words in a language all our own, dreaming dreams, making promises, conquering worlds side by side, and in the autumn she was gone. Gone with the wood thrushes and the tanagers, gone with the phoebes and the orioles. Gone back to her home in Virginia, where she was struck down and killed only a few weeks later, walking along the highway on her way home from school. Her last loving, longing letter reached me a day later.

In that black and hollow autumn too came the beginning of the long dying of the Lord's Woods. And I found out what *mourning* means.

# THIRTEEN

# The Living

No ONE COULD PRETEND that until autumn the woods were undefiled; that everywhere in this green and graceful oasis primeval beauty was preserved immaculate. There at its heart was the smokestack of the waterworks (the shorter square-snouted original one was still standing, but now the smoke curled from a tapering cylindrical stack that towered above it), spewing down its acrid folds of soft-coal smoke, and all around the grimy red-brick Victorian building with the pumping sounds forever coming from it were heaped and scattered the litter of the business: the field full of rusting sections of pipe we called the Pipe Farm, shacks and sheds for tools, the railroad trestle with cones of coal under it, discarded cement mixers, wheelbarrows, chains, an ancient truck or two, parked forever. But all this mess was concentrated, and it was the price we had to pay, apparently, to have the woods exist at all.

There was, as well, the debris and the refuse of poverty and slovenliness along its southern border, where all the streets dead-ended, and the neighbors just tossed away everything they'd squeezed the last ounce of usefulness or value out of.

There was the boy scout campground, with its fairy ring of bottles and tin cans and its widening field of frayed, three-foot stumplings. And blaze marks on every tree on every trail in every direction.

There were the hunters and their guns, and overhead the blatting of the Curtiss Robins and Wacos and the Stearmans. But all these invasions and desecrations left the woods still supreme, still remote and wild, secret and mysterious, still more a place for Ovenbird and Veery, for cottontail and raccoon than for man. You could still enter the Green Cathedral at the end of Westwood Road, and walk the aisle of swamp maples along the Cinder Road, through the marsh under the willows, across the Stone Bridge, right on to the waterworks, and then follow the wide pipe-line path all the way back to the Old Gray Road and the farms beyond; you could go there on any summer afternoon, on any spring morning, and not see another human being, unless you happened to run into Roy or Bud or Howie. Or beat along any path of all the hundreds that crisscrossed the woods and walk smack into a dew-spangled spider's web that no one else had shattered. Or sprawl under a tree in that glade in the Big Woods and study Latin or read Shakespeare and listen to the flies zooming in the sun and drowse with no one ever to disturb you. And you could, in every copse and thicket and around every twisting of every stream, believe that this was the way it looked to the first colonists, and before them to the Indians, and before them to the deer, the moose, the bear, and the wild turkey.

The water that flowed down Teal Stream and Foster's Brook was still so clean you could see the little killies and the baby perch and pickerel in the shadows of Three Bridges or the logs along Stepping Stone Island, and the air was so clear you could almost stretch out your hand and touch the towers of the city, wavering there across the marsh. At night, the skies were peppered thick with stars.

Countless days, countless nights, hours without number we had seen these woods, in every season, in every wind and weather: in spring filled with birds like a carnival, in winter black and creaking and empty. Almost every tree had a meaning or a memory:

here we sat that time we formed the smoking club, back in fifth grade, with a pack of Melachrinos and a bottle of Listerine for camouflage. It didn't work and we all got thrashed, or anyway, I did. And there we slept one night, with pup tent and mess kit and can of beans, but forgot the bug repellent. There by Teal Stream those goofy boys (my brother Richard among them) said they found strange clues and a piece of human flesh carved from a thigh by a Chinese scimitar! When the police, almost as foolish, came back with them to investigate, they analyzed the human flesh as half a loaf of white bread and went away disgusted (or disappointed).

There by the red clay ditch was the little grove of sweet gums Carl and I called Warblers Saplings, with a deliberate double plural so that we would say it slowly and savor forever that spring morning tumultuous with Magnolia, Canada, and Blackpoll Warblers.

Here near the boy scout camp was the tree where Ben found the possum hanging by his tail, and over behind the cattail marsh lived the weasel, known only to George, and never seen by us. And just off the Grassy Road was a glade where, one day, we watched a family of flying squirrels dive and sweep from tree to tree, more daring aerialists even than the swift gray squirrels. There was the Indian Tree, still crouched over Jewelweed Stream, there was Anne's Tree, and near it the oak where the little gray squirrel was buried. Pussy willows where the hummingbird nested beside Stepping Stone Island, swampy glade of the Prothonotary Warbler, Washington's barge out on the marsh, and Musky the mink in the old water boiler.

Trees hallowed by a hundred kinds of birds that had stopped there to glow briefly in a shaft of sunlight, to sing, and then move on.

Up Teal Stream toward the railroad track, where it was wide and the banks, was the spot where someone had hung a stout rope from an overhanging sweet gum, and we swung across, for years, like Tarzan. Here, at this same spot one day in early spring, the stream was filled chock full of little eels; first spring elvers, all wriggling upstream against the current, each no more than five inches long, thick as a pencil, swimming by the millions, in from the sea, all the way from Bermuda!

Here, too hidden to most of the intruders, lay the forest glade in the heart of the Thrush Woods where I found the Ovenbird's nest that afternoon in May when I was supposed to be playing right field at baseball practice. Standing out there on the field motionless and bored, hearing the warblers singing at the wood's edge, inching further and further to the right, to the boundary of the field. Fnally vanishing behind the hedge of the school tennis courts at the moment all eyes were on a close play at home plate. Hotfooting it down the Cinder Road, mitt flung into a thicket. "Coach," said Beano to Rolfe, when the team came in to bat. "I think we're missing our right fielder. Arbib's disappeared." "Damn it, he's done it again," said Rolfe Humphries, who took his baseball and his poetry seriously.

It was the same glade that Ben would remember, years later, having escaped to it when the clamor at home grew overwhelming. (There were four boys growing up in the little house on Wood Lane.) "I would go and sit on a log in the darkening glade. Listen to the Wood Thrushes singing from the shadowy woods. Sitting motionless there until it was dark and the last faraway thrush had sent up his last note. Then I would feel calm again."

It was still there.

Westward from the old barge, now bottomless and filled with algae-scummy green water were salt meadows that still stretched unbroken all the way to the abandoned railway trestle and beyond. Here I had toiled alone one entire summer, collecting brackish water fish for J. T. Nichols, Curator of Recent (geologically speaking) Fishes at the museum. Slogging across the meadows from slough to creek to ditch, lugging seines and net traps and bait (stale cake) and knapsack and canteen and, of course, binoculars. Sliding hip-deep in black ooze, struggling out only to slither into another slippery-sided slough. Legs and arms pocked with mosquito and fly bites, face shiny with sweat and streaked with mud. Getting to know the creatures of the marsh. Following the mouse tracks, finding the muskrat houses, locating the colonies of marsh wren nests and learning which were occupied and which had been built merely for practice or for exhibition. Taking the small fish as they hung motionless over the baited nets—the killifish and the fingerlings of the larger species. Learning how this seeming empty marshland teemed with living things of value, all interdependent and each important. And all the while the Black-billed Cuckoos looked down, floating their tremulous chants from the towering oaks of the hummocks out over the sea of grass and the lone toiler there, bent over seine and line and notebook. It was all still there.

# FOURTEEN

# Beginning

THEN ONE DAY, just by the Range, I found a cluster of narrow wooden stakes, tacked into the ground, and some little flagsticks, the kind surveyors used, some with chalk markings on them—numbers in blue. Oh Christ, I thought, not another hole and another well, just here under Anne's Tree! And then looking down the Range, saw a hundred yards away another cluster. Ran down to look at them in panic. And saw, through the binoculars, across the marsh, marching into the distance like an even-spaced phalanx of Caesar's army, a column of white stakes, some with flags flying, westward across the salt marsh. And stood and wondered, feeling sick, what kind of a road they would bring, or perhaps a railway track, or a highway, or hopefully as the least menacing, a buried pipe line.

I walked back to the Cinder Road and saw that there were other clusters off in the woods to the east, swinging around to run eastward, just parallel to the southern boundary of the woods, perhaps a hunderd yards north of it. Between the clusters of stakes someone had slashed swaths of underbrush and even some small trees, leaving them wilting and dying where they fell. Sassafras and highbush blueberry and here and there an oak sapling. And one dogwood. Butchered.

Then quickly retraced the path between the stakes, furiously pulling them up one by one, straining, cursing, half mad in a

147

frenzy of despair and outrage. Heaving them out of the soft ground and tossing them as far as I could fling them into the underbrush, kicking off the ones that could not be pulled. Raging through the woods, along the Range, and out into the marsh, crying havoc in my heart for whatever evil was coming, knowing this act of fury was senseless and in the end would be futile.

They put the stakes back in the ground the next week, and when we tried to walk through, along the Cinder Road, there was a workman sitting guard beside the Indian Tree who told us to go back, the woods were closed.

I asked him why, and then heard the worst: a power line was coming through, and they were starting construction on the towers. There'd been some dirty work, he told us, a whole week's surveying work destroyed! We shook our heads sympathetically and went around the other way, sneaking in along Teal Stream, and spent the afternoon like conspirators crouched in the deepest part of the Lady's Slipper Grove, waiting. The new stakes were all pulled and flung and broken before midnight.

I suppose it gave us some small satisfaction that we were fighting this monstrous invasion in the only way we knew, but we knew it was a token resistance in a battle we could not win. A delaying action only, and to no avail. The concrete platforms were set into the ground with a clang of machinery and a cluttering of sand and gravel, and new truck ruts all through the underbrush. Slowly (but how swiftly!) the steel towers rose above the platforms, their tops high above the tallest oaks, and then the cables were strung, looping across marsh, down the Range, and then down the middle of the hideous gash, a hundred and fifty feet wide, they cleared right through the Big Woods.

And no one, except those few of us, complained. It was all done without discussion, with no more than passing mention in the local newspaper, with no one knowing what was planned until it happened. Like a *coup d'état!* like hunter against rabbit, with no warning and no reprieve. When it became known—not until the work was well along—that a power line, with high steel towers, was sweeping across the marsh and through the Lord's Woods, there was, if anything, general approval. Better through that waste land than across our village, down our street, over our garden. The land, after all, belonged to the water company; it was theirs to lease or sell or give easements as they wished. Those woods will be gone some day anyway. You can't fight progress.

We took it hard; to us it was a personal tragedy, and an omen. Suddenly the wide treeless clearing with the terrifying steel monsters overhead became a vision of the future: the woods defenseless and with no protector, to be mutilated, defaced, raped, and then destroyed by anyone who wanted it, and who could pay for it and make a profit. Oh, they could announce that less than five per cent of all the wooded area had been cut down. But now gone was that green tunnel and its magic at the entrance, the deepening mystery and silence and sanctuary of the Green Cathedral. Now, just past the bend at the Indian Tree, you came out into bright sunlight and dry, barren no man's land, under the menace of the towers. It was all wrong; it was a desecration. But in time we became accustomed to it, and years later had to think a minute to remember exactly which trees had been here and were now gone, and how it had looked then. Under the power lines the underbrush grew back: catbrier and blueberry, sassafras and bracken, and Yellowthroats and Catbirds moved in.

But standing and waiting, lonely and lovely, the rest of the Lord's Woods lived on.

Slowly, but inevitably, the Bird Club began to break up. By ones and twos its members were graduated from school and went off to college, and somehow they were never replaced. During the club's brief heyday no effort at active recruitment had been made—indeed, the group was so close-knit, with such a mystique about its activities and such a fierce dedication that it became almost impossible to find candidates (actually it was the other way around, for we had never looked for any), and few additions to the original group of friends were made.

Roy had gone off to Yale to prepare to become a doctor in his father's footsteps. The following autumn Bob followed him to Yale, Howie began at Bowdoin, and Andy left for Wabash. Fin and Bud, who had earlier departed for a boarding school in

# The Lord's Woods

Massachusetts began at college the following year, and that year—the September after Anne's death—I joined Roy and Bob at Yale (it was Dave Harrower's current recommendation for biology), while Duke's choice was Columbia.

Dave himself departed for a year's sabbatical, seeking his doctorate in ornithology at Cornell, and lacking his guiding spirit, the club seemed to falter.

Ben was the club's last official president, and the last active members were Tommy, Andy's brother Roddy, Tommy's classmate Eddie, and Dave's son, young Dave. The Friday evening meetings were losing their inviolability and some were even cancelled. Finally, the clubroom in Roy's father's basement was closed down, the battered Saw-whet Owl disappeared, as did the equally disreputable gull-bartered Studer.

Two volumes of *The Heron* had been proudly published, each a handsome forty-page journal, well printed on laid paper, with photographs and an attractive cover. *The Heron* had taught us how to organize our thinking in a written document for publication, it had acted as an incentive to our studies and in club activities, it had brought us a moment of fame (favorable reviews in the New York *Sun*, *Bird Lore*, and *Nature Magazine*), and perhaps best of all, given us that delicious thrill of seeing our own names above a page of printed type.

No one ever kept count of how many meetings had been held in that cellar room, or if they did, the record is gone with the carefully transcribed minutes of the meetings. In the two years before the last *Heron*, the count was thirty-seven, so it must be supposed that the club gathered more than a hundred times there on Friday evenings, and countless other times in smaller groups, unofficially—at the Lord Estate, at the bay's edge, or in the woods.

Although it was the woods that was our heart's home and our life's pivot, our search for new discoveries led us out in ever-widening circles. At first it was to places we could reach by walking or by bicycle: our bay, Atlantic Beach, Rosedale Pond, Valley Stream park. Later in Dave's car and then by various family cars the excursions spread: Hempstead Reservoir and

# Beginning

Jones Beach, Mill Neck and the North Shore. And still farther away, to Carman's River, Montauk and Orient eastward on the island, and to Cape May, and Cobb's Island on the Virginia Coast.

The year I joined the club we had held our first Christmas Count, an all-day bird-counting race, with eight of us in Dave's car or on bicycles. It rained all day, and we were soaked and chilled long before the daylight waned and we gathered at the good teacher's house for hot chocolate and ginger snaps and to add up the total. We were tired too: we had dashed from the bay at dawn and the woods just after daylight to Jones Beach and back to Wantagh, Long Beach, and Valley Stream, ending at the woods again where we had started. The total was 11,243 individual birds, comprising 45 different species. And although the club ceased to exist formally when Ben joined the gang at Yale, it remained alive in our minds, and its members were always "the Bird Club," or "Dave's Boys." Whenever we came home for school holidays or for summer vacations, we came together in the same informal ways, walked the woods together, or went out on morning excursions to more distant hunting grounds. And every Christmas joined in the year's one great bird-watching orgy, the Christmas Count. It is continued to this day.

In those days the club members were our closest friends, and most of our excursions were in their company, but our circle of bird-watching friends was rapidly growing. One reason was the fame we had brought to the woods themselves by our publication of *The Heron*, and by the records we were now submitting to *Bird Lore Magazine*. Another was the mimeographed publication that Dave started before he went off to Cornell, a weekly newsletter that he named *Long Island Bird Notes*. Quickly every ardent bird watcher on the island became both a contributor and a subscriber, sending to Dave, on each Tuesday, their discoveries of the preceding week, receiving, the following Saturday a bulletin on what had arrived, departed, who had seen what and where. Suddenly the little bird club group became a part of an island-wide coterie. There was Doctor Will Helmuth in East Hampton, Roy Latham in Orient, LeRoy Wilcox in Speonk, Gil Raynor in Manorville, a whole crowd in northern Queens

# The Lord's Woods

County, George Rose in Mineola, John Mayer roaming the Idlewild marshes, John Elliott in Seaford, Ralph Lind and Bob Rorden and the Smithe brothers on the North Shore and Geoffrey Gill in Huntington, and one bona fide scientist of great renown, John T. Nichols of Garden City, my fish mentor.

Each week for almost three years *Bird Notes* brought news and a sense of cameraderie to the scattered correspondents. And now, when we sped out to eastern Suffolk County we might stop along the way to say hello to Doc Helmuth or Roy Wilcox, and sometimes join them in the field. One summer, when Dave was off exploring somewhere, he left the *Bird Notes* in Bud's care, and mine. The correspondents got a new mailing address and the mimeograph machine was installed in my cellar atop the ping-pong table. And though we had fearful production problems (we never properly learned how to operate the blasted machine), we managed to send forth each week, to the thirty-five subscribers, including two museums, our somewhat smudged, infinitely less formal bulletin. When Bud went off to Maine later in the summer I had it all to myself, an editor at last!

Two years later, when Dave had tired of it, he bequeathed me the *Bird Notes* and shortly afterward I induced a local newspaper to run it as a weekly column. Thereafter, each Friday, without a single interval for more than twenty years, the *Long Island Bird Notes* appeared before an audience of tens of thousands. But my own part in it was minor. After thirty months, or 130 columns, I was invited to join the armed forces, and John Elliott took over, "temporarily." He kept it going for seventeen years, and those columns, mine and his were in effect a window on the world of birds and conservation for our island and served to introduce hundreds of new believers to our religion.

Through all those years you can find, if you search the newspaper files, bird records followed by the initials WW, standing for Woodmere Woods, and followed by other initials, the observers: DDB, RWB, BCB, RW, HV, RB, RA—Dave's Boys—and the newer visitors too: GR, JM, ADC. For the Lord's Woods, under whatever name anyone chose to give them, were still in any season a magic place, filled with birds and beauty.

# FIFTEEN

# Storm

THE DAY HAD BEGUN ominously, with an oppressive heaviness in the air, an exhausting, humid, hanging closeness that could suffocate; the air was like the bottom of a fish tank. By half past nine in the morning a solid gray overcast had rolled across the sky, high up, but under it smoke-dark, ragged clouds scudded at low levels, moving fast, resolving in wild, wierd shapes and then quickly dissolving. It was the kind of day when anything could happen: a manic murder, a suicide, the strangling of a little child. More than likely, it would bring a thunderstorm by late afternoon.

Threatening sky or not, I had to go into the city that morning, to be interviewed for a job. I parked my ancient secondhand Plymouth on a maple-shaded side street in Jamaica and caught the shiny new E train to Manhattan. When I reached the city, the sky was even more menacing, darker now at the southern horizon, as if some horrible black monster was crouched there, just beyond the curve of the world, waiting to engulf the city.

The appointment was brief; there was no job. A New York newspaper had just died, and three hundred experienced newspaper men were out begging for work, any work, for as little as fifteen dollars a week. It seemed that always, at every office I visited, they were always there ahead of me. With infinitely more experience, and with families to feed. So I went once again to the library, to look through the *Times* classifieds and through the business directories for some new names to write letters to, asking for an interview. When I walked down the wide steps of the library, a little after noon, I knew that I had to get home without delay, because something strange and terrifying was about to happen. The heat and the suffocating humidity seemed to have increased, and the sky was so dark now and so curiously green, that it could only be moments before the storm. It was as if the sky were sick and would soon go into convulsions. The city seemed to be waiting, holding its breath, moving quietly under a dark and fearful spell. There was no wind, and no leaf stirred.

When I came up the subway stairs at Jamaica, the wind had sprung up, already strong and wet, and the maple trees were rolling in it. Clouds of dust and litter whirled up from the gutters, and the light was crepuscular and green. Eerie. Then the rain came; a few fat drops at first, sending me running to the car, and then a sudden burst that blew slanting across the streets and the wildly heaving trees.

With every mile I drove, the storm mounted in violence. The winds increased until it was hard to believe that such fury could be possible. The rain blew down in sheets, now hard, now twice as hard, now almost explosively. Through the streets of South Jamaica everything movable was moving; through the rain-blurred windshield I could see hanging storefront signs swinging insanely, trees tossing, paper and leaves flying, and all the wires on the street poles swinging as for some giant's skiprope game. It would be safer, surely, once I reached the turnpike and the open marshland. But then I had to stop the car to get out and pry a flying sheet of newspaper from the windshield, and as I crouched, fighting the wind and getting drenched, a round white light globe, big as a basketball, left the pole across the street and sailed down to shatter at my feet.

The world of the storm was abandoned to me; nowhere along the way was man, child, or car moving.

When I reached the turnpike across the marsh, the storm had

154

reached its peak of cataclysmic fury. The rains streamed across the landscape horizontally. The highway had all but disappeared and the bay moved in to reclaim it; wide pools—lakes—of tidewater and rain had flooded all the low places; I had to guess from poles and signs where the roadway was in all that water. Suddenly, ahead of me, a giant roadside billboard took flight, cartwheeling like a busted airplane wing across the road and into the marsh. Then up ahead, another sailed across the road, and behind me, just missing me, a third.

I had to fight to keep the little car on course in winds that heaved and battered it, and our progress was that of a weaving drunk. Off on the right, towards the bay, some telephone poles had fallen, and their wires flapped in tangled disarray. One of the little squatter's shacks that stood out on the marsh on piles had lost its roof, and all the others were awash and being pounded by wind-whipped waves. Small signs flew through the air, and a few gulls blew out of nowhere and disappeared. On the diner beside Hook Creek the hanging Eat sign had been folded neatly back against the roof, its heavy pipe supports bent double.

It was all wildly exciting. I was surprised to find myself awed and exhilarated by the screeching wind, the driving rain, the menacing sky, the flooded marsh, and all this riot of the elements. To be out all alone in it, to move against this raging, ravaging force, to feel it pummel the car, to find myself leaning against it, moving through it, breathing miraculously in all this flying water, with the heightened danger from the sailing billboards and the whipping wires. The storm filled the bowl of the sky and the world below with howling chaos. It was tumult. It was peril. It was tremendous.

I made it home, snaking through the village streets, a welter of fallen trees and branches, downed wires and mountains of leaves wrenched from their branches. To find my father trying to shore up the screen porch with some oars from the garage and lamenting the loss of three ornamental spruces. The house was dark, the telephones dead, there was a foot of water in the cellar. My family was astonished to see me; they had assumed I would stay in the city until the hurricane had passed.

# The Lord's Woods

"Hurricane?" I asked, surprised (delighted). The word had never even entered my mind. New York had never had a hurricane, that anyone could remember. Who said it was a hurricane?

That's what everyone was calling it. On the radio before the electricity was cut off. But no one could understand where it had come from; how it had come upon us with this violence, and no warning.

Early in the evening the winds, which had been out of the east, then the north, shifted to the west, and the rains slackened and then died, and finally the black sky rolled up at the edges and just before dark, turned orange. I lay awake for a long time that night, thinking about the storm, my foolhardy journey through it, and thought more about the devastation to the wildlife; all those marsh animals flooded out of their homes, all those birds out unprotected. And finally thought about the woods. I would have to go there in the morning, but would go in trepidation and fear, knowing that no good could have come from this ill-starred day.

It was worse than I had feared. The woods had been ravaged and left lying in shambles. As I walked up the Cinder Road from the Range, I came to a green, impassable abatis of tumbled wreckage. The tall oaks had lost some giant limbs; some had crashed to the ground and others were torn and hanging, but it was the red maples of the Thrush Woods that had been devastated. On both sides of the Cinder Road the woods were now a lake, with maples toppled in all directions, as if they had been sent flying by some Olympian bowling ball. The wide, flat masses of shallow roots had been torn out of the black earth and now stood vertical, dripping mud, contorted as if in agony. Everywhere was a heaped confusion of tumbled foliage; whole tree crowns, branches, leaves. I had to fight my way along the Cinder Road, now climbing over a fallen tree trunk, now crawling under another, now clawing my way through the dense upper branches of a third. It seemed to me that at least one of every three trees along the Green Cathedral had been uprooted and now lay flat or stood leaning against other trees, ready to fall with the next strong wind.

# Storm

But this was not the worst shock. When I reached the bend in the road, just past the clump of Hercules'-club we prized as such a rarity, the woods had simply vanished. Here by Stepping Stone Island every tree was down in one vast brush heap! Gone was the glade of pussy willow where the Ruby-throated Hummingbird nested beside Teal Stream year after year. Down were the trees where our treasured Yellow-crowned Night Heron roosted each spring; even the high trees that walled in the cattail marsh were piled in awful disarray, and the willow alley, though it still survived, hung maimed and broken, forever disfigured. Teal Stream was over its banks and indeed over Three Bridges; the Stone Bridge was almost awash. The waters of the stream now ran fast and dark brown.

Bud was standing at the Stone Bridge, shaking his head. We stood silently, as if at a wake, looking around us at our beautiful woods, now lying in ruin, drowned, battered, beaten; never in our lifetimes would they be as lovely as they had been before this storm. "Gad, Bibs," was all that he could say, and he said it over and over again. I felt as if someone had kicked me viciously in the pit of my stomach. I wanted to howl in protest, but I was too numb, stunned with this disaster that had blown up out of nowhere, as unexpected, and as chilling, as the news of Anne's death, which still had me aching, five years later. We wondered what had become of all the marsh animals: the marshes were still flooded—broad lakes that seemed to stretch straight across to the abandoned railway trestle. Perhaps it was a hurricane that had brought Washington's Barge across the marshes to its final resting place, for when the waters finally receded, the salt marsh was littered with windows of sea wrack and driftwood, with here and there a battered rowboat or a broken packing crate, or just driftwood high and dry on the salt meadows.

We found a dead night heron, and strangely, perhaps, a Bonaparte's Gull torn and broken and far from the open ocean where he belonged. But living birds were all around us, quiet but active in the brush and in the trees. At least that was a good sign; the woods were not forsaken entirely—not yet, anyway.

It took the waterworks crew months to make the Cinder Road

passable again and to clear the wreckage from the Grassy Road along the pipe line. But the trees that had fallen back in the woods and around the cattail marsh were left lying where they fell. Some clung to life for years, sending up shoots in new directions so that foliage grew from the upper side of the trunk like a green mane. Some died quickly, and some lingered for a few years and then gave up. Their slowly rotting hulks lay buried in the black mud and blacker pools across the Thrush Woods. But the jagged holes in the forest canopy now let the sun in and dispelled the mystery. The Wood Thrushes disappeared, as did the Ovenbirds, the Black-and-white Warblers, and the pair of nuthatches that always nested just inside the woods at the edge of the big marsh. For years afterward this would be a silent, almost deserted forest, an empty house with all the children gone, with holes in the roof and the walls tumbling down.

But all was not lost. Slowly, one by one, other creatures found their way into this part of the woods. Towhees and robins and catbirds moved in, and a pair of flickers, and phoebes came to nest against the upturned maple roots, and Red-eyed Vireos sang loud on summer mornings. The surviving maples leafed out and flourished with less competition, and some of the smaller trees of the forest understory began to fill the empty spaces. It would take a lifetime, but the Green Cathedral, if left alone, could repair itself. It was still a place of beauty, a wilderness, a joy.

It was the woods on the west of the road, beyond the bend, where all was changed and would never be the same again. Here was nothing but a mountainous sea of impenetrable brush, with tree trunks scattered like jackstraws and not a tall tree spared. The following spring the slow invasion began, of catbrier, poison ivy, wild grape, blackberry; before long you could not enter this wild dominion from any side. For a time it lay there silent and empty, brooding and open to the sky, and then a new bird population invested it. Thrashers and yellowthroats, White-eyed Vireos and Song Sparrows, and even a pair of Kingbirds that used the one naked tree stub as a perch. The cottontails and smaller rodents must have loved this sea of tangle; no hunter could beat his way through it, or even see into it. But it was not the woods we knew.

For the remainder, the woods had withstood the mighty hurricane with little damage. Gradually, we grew accustomed to the new scenes that greeted us, noted with satisfaction the way the birds and animals were adapting to the changes and filling in empty niches in the altered environment. We loved the woods no less now: a virgin daughter despoiled but still beloved, still cherished.

But now we felt the aching foreboding of disaster. First, there had been the power lines. And then the hurricane. What next?

# SIXTEEN

# Invasion

In TRUTH, we knew what the next catastrophe would likely be. We tried not to think about it, as if by closing our minds to it we could somehow make it disappear. But it was on the map, and everyone knew that someday it would happen.

It was called Peninsula Boulevard, and people said that it would eventually link the turnpike on the west with the Sunrise Highway to the north. No one could say precisely where it would be located, but we knew it would run through the Lord Estate and into the woods. When we protested to each other and anyone else who would listen that there were already three major roads that paralleled this route we were reminded that since the boulevard would be cut through marsh and undeveloped lands and woodland for much of its length, and would be straight and wide, it would serve to keep the trucks and other traffic out of West Broadway (which was narrow and dangerous), Broadway, and Central Avenue, and thus out of the residential streets of our villages. "All the state needs is the money," warned my father, ominously. "They've been talking about that highway for twenty years."

We knew that it was planned. We hated to be reminded of it. It hung there, a Damoclean sword, sickening to think of, and so not to be thought of. We lived with that projected boulevard as if it were a dormant plague that lingered deep in our bones, a constant malaise that would some day flare up and strike us down. Secretly praying and silently hoping that this monstrous unthinkable eventuality, like death itself, would not come soon; would remain unrealized forever, or at least until we were older, could organize our opposition, and somehow expunge it from the map. But all the time it lurked there, ready to strike, like the power line, like the hurricane, without any real warning. Its very threat heightened our awareness of the woods, now flawed along its southern edge and at its heart, but still precious.

Some years earlier, work had actually started on the boulevard, with a two-lane concrete street laid down that knifed through the marshes eastward from the turnpike and then dead-ended in the Lord Estate. Nothing much had ever happened along it but the addition of a few houses and a lot of rubbish, and each summer the battalions of phragmites crowded a little closer to the concrete, regaining their territory, perhaps some day to recapture it entirely. We had almost forgotten that the western stub of the boulevard was the first step in the plan—an arrow aimed at our hearts.

Then it happened, with a swiftness that amazed us. This time we had advance warning. The local newspaper first announced that funds had been made available, and that the long-planned highway would soon become a reality. The story made it sound like the marvel of the age. It would be a wide, modern, banked ribbon of concrete, two lanes wide at first and eventually four, ideally located in mostly undeveloped tracts. It would serve to divert a major share of the trucking and much automobile traffic from our narrow village streets. It was another welcome sign that our area was growing, expanding, preparing for the future, moving forward with America. It was progress. It would slice straight through the water company's woodlands.

We watched and waited, sick inside and helpless as each succeding announcement fell upon us like the lashes of doom. There was an invitation for contractors to submit bids. There was a formal opening of bids. The contract was awarded. And finally,

# Invasion

the news that the project would begin without delay. No complaint was raised by anyone. It was much too late for that.

No surprises this time. Within a few weeks you could go down to the older stretch of the road, where it had come to a dead end in the Lord Estate, and see all the paraphernalia and clutter of progress. We knew the routine now. The phragmites and the jewelweed, the spicebush and the birch flattened and the stakes set into the ground. Then day by day the slow, desperately final obliteration. First the bulldozers crashing the trees to the ground, shouldering them aside, converting them in hours from graceful green into tormented heaps of refuse. Then the ground pushed around, graded flat, and then the rollers smoothing, the gravel and cinders spread, the rollers again, the concrete poured, smoothed, set. We knew it all: the noise, the litter, the welter of men and equipment, the dust, the oil drums with their smoking trash fires, and finally the broad ribbons of concrete creeping across the land, creeping closer, ever closer to our woods. It was a monster that could not be halted; an endless concrete reptile that fed on trees and flowers and left as its vomit and its excreta, this barren, white wasteland. Felled and crunched and flattened and killed, leaving in its wake hot white rock, eight inches thick. Taking with it trees that had sprung from seeds and acorns dropped on that black soil a hundred years or more earlier, seeds that had been, perhaps, tromped into the ground by a deer, or brought there from some distant place by migratory birds. Flattening the oaks and maples and beeches and hickory alike, tumbling the willows and alder and birch and poplar, sealing the rabbit warrens and the fox dens and the holes of the meadow mice and the wet swales where the woodcock lay. Unselecting, unsparing, and conclusive.

It came down through the phragmites east of us and roared into the open groves of white oaks in the Lord Estate, with a crashing of huge trees and a grinding of bulldozers. It went right through Mr. Rieffer's back garden, where so many moths had been collected on summer nights. It drove through the subdivision, down between Heller's and the old red-brick mansion where the squatters had lived and took down the oak where Ben and I had discovered our first Brewster's Warbler. Now all those half-forgotten streets of the subdivision with their faded signs and grassy margins were suddenly cloven by a highway and brought back into the world again. It skirted the southern end of the golf course without touching it, and then like the upraised knife, it was at the very throat of the woods.

The surveyors' lanes were cut through the woods, and when we saw where they led, we sighed, as much in relief as in sorrow. For though the boulevard would cross the entire length of the Lord's Woods, it would transect the southern boundary only, parallel and south of the power line, taking out that strip of woodland already separated by the tall towers and the clearing below. That strip, already isolated, with the mean streets and the rubbish at regular intervals along it, would have been our choice for the highway, if it had come to a choice.

Even so, the devastation was appalling. Gone would be the tiny pond where that enormous snapping turtle surfaced that day so long ago, and where it surely lurked for half a century. The orchard behind Quinn's old farmhouse would be obliterated and with it the entire curve of the Cinder Road. The farmhouse, once remote and hidden on its backwoods road, would now perch at the very edge of the highway, if it survived at all. The giant spruce trees where we found the Long-eared Owl would disappear, as would the woodcock hollow (our first woodcock!), the Indian Tree, and the stream where the fox left his spoor in the snow. Even that impenetrable old thicket that always sheltered in winter a Brown Thrasher or a Catbird—all would be leveled. The entire length of the south side of the woods—white oaks, hickories, ashes, maples, and sweet gums which had flourished here for centuries—would be no more.

They hacked and cleared and flattened, and carved, where all had been green and whispering, a wide and empty canyon stretching straight into the distance. And then they stopped. Unaccountably, the workmen hauled away their equipment and vanished, leaving the eastern section of the highway unpaved and useless. Now traffic could speed down a smooth road all the way from the turnpike to a point just west of Quinn's house, and then come to a dead end with a sawhorse barrier. There, for several years, "progress" stood in abeyance.

But not in abeyance everywhere. For years, a slow transition had been taking place in the Lord Estate. Now and then, at great intervals in time and place, a house was built on one of those all-but-abandoned plots. First to be invaded were those fields where the auction itself had been held, but when the boulevard was cut through, new houses began to appear along its length. Around each house a plot of marsh was cleared and filled, lawn and shrubbery planted, and a few birds and animals moved away. One by one the dusty grass lanes with the proud names that had been empty and deserted years before acquired resident home-owners; with the houses came highway crews to fill and repair, to replace culverts that had collapsed, to make things passable for people and for cars. And put back the street signs.

There was still far more vacant land than was occupied, and this was everywhere untouched and unchanged. We discovered that the birds—at least the migrants passing through—had no objections to the occasional houses and gardens, as long as the treetops still bloomed. Along the tall oak streets back of Heller's each spring, the migration flooded the leafy canopy on both sides of the boulevard. Now exposed, inhabited, frequented later in the day by delivery boys and postman, no longer a secret of the club, but right there in someone's back yard!

I have no memory of the completion of Peninsula Boulevard through the Lord's Woods. I was away from home for five years on the more urgent business of the United States Army. I know the highway was completed a year or two after I left, but in the thoughts of it which were a part of the soldier's burden of memories, I had blotted out the recent catastrophes; the salt marshes, the Lord Estate, the woods, and the farms to the north all reverted to their earlier innocence and sustained me.

When I returned at last, it was not to the same Lord's Woods. The boulevard with its new easy access and its long southern perimeter, brought newer and more persistent dumping. Along both sides of the highways was strewn the ugly detritus of suburban living. Here a painter had dumped his empty pails and a dozen remnant rolls of wallpaper. There was a moldering truckload of paper boxes. Gardeners were the worst offenders; the road was disfigured along its length by heaps of decaying grass, prunings, and garden rubbish. Now and then a clump of blackberry or giant ragweed revealed in its heart a rotting armchair, or a pile of tin cans, or an ancient overcoat. There seemed no way to prevent or even discourage this outrage to decency and to beauty: litterers are like burglars; they do their dirty work when everyone else sleeps.

Worse, because it was inside the woods itself, was the Range. Now the beautiful white oaks that remained on either side of the power lines towers looked down on a battlefield of refuse. No more was this a place echoing to the Bluebirds and the Killdeer and the Rose-breasted Grosbeak, or a place to search for wildflowers, or to come by night and murmur words of love; the Range was now a place to back up your pickup truck and let fly with whatever it was that was too much trouble to carry to the community dump. The water company put up large signs forbidding dumping, but they were soon shot full of holes, and then knocked over, and finally buried under garbage. And, as if to celebrate the new condition of the Range, a half dozen Starlings took up shrieking residence.

Something else had happened besides the litter and the loss of field and woodland. There was a loss of remoteness. Before the highway, there had only been one easy entrance to the woods from our village, the Cinder Road with its concealed access at the end of Westwood Road. Oh, yes, if you wanted to beat your way through thickets and marshy places you could walk down any of those dead-end streets east of Westwood, but almost no one ever did. Now, with the broad highway running its entire length, access was there for anyone who passed, a green inviting place that could be seen for the first time by strangers and passers-by; suddenly discovered by hundreds of people who had lived nearby all their lives and had never known this fascinating place existed, or how to enter it. Discovered too by others who lived far away but saw in passing a place to stop and investigate, steal a bush, slash a tree, kill a rabbit, dump some rubbish, run a dog, or more rarely to walk quietly and with respect.

Now exposed with roaring traffic along one edge; smaller by half a hundred acres, with the menace of the overhanging towers, our woods had a new frontier. Beaten back, pillaged, and desecrated, this southern boundary was now the power line, the boulevard a double barrier of ugliness. But you could stop your car anywhere along the highway, pull it off onto the grassy shoulder, and beat through hot thickets under the power line and enter the woods. Still cool and dark, serene and green. The Green Cathedral still soared over the Cinder Road, the two secret glades had been somehow spared, the Grassy Road and Teal Stream and Stepping Stone Island, the cattail marsh and Warblers Saplings and the Deep Ditch and the Thrush Woods were all still intact. Showing the scars of that first hurricane, and a second one two years ago, but still, as ever, a green wilderness oasis in a fast-changing world. You could still lie on your back over the water at Three Bridges and hear the same Blue-winged Warbler (or a descendant) buzzing from the crown of the same white oak, and you could fall asleep there and sleep all afternoon with no one to disturb you. Still feel the sense of sanctuary and serenity. But now, on summer Sundays there were more people in the woods than ever before: children running and shouting, older boys in vandalpacks, strolling men and women, and romping, baying dogs. There were other bird watchers, too, lured by the fame we brought to this place, come from faraway to walk our paths and share our dicoveries.

Perhaps at last, we thought, as our woods entered this new era, the slings and arrows were all spent, and the outrageous turns of fortune were behind us. The best part of the woods still survived, and the waterworks would always remain here, guarding its watershed and its wells. We could see the beginning of the end for the Lord Estate. The golf course, abandoned for the second time, might eventually disappear, and the farms. But the woods and the salt marsh would go on forever. Or so we earnestly believed. But we knew, deep in our hearts, that the story was not ended, and wondered what new disaster might await us.

167

# SEVENTEEN

# Fire

I<small>T WAS FIRE</small>.

How or where it started, no one could tell. Throughout the history of the woods—of any woodland—there will be unimportant fires from time to time, occasionally a major conflagration caused by lightning or by man. In the Lord's Woods we had come to expect sporadic minor fires. Usually they broke out in autumn when the ground and the fallen foliage were dry. Some picnicker or hunter or youthful litter-gang would leave a cigarette or campfire smoldering and it would spread through a patch of underbrush, eating its way through a glade or copse and then be discovered and doused by the waterworks crew, or the volunteer firemen, or even by members of the club. It would leave a blackened wound all winter, a few dead bushes and a scarred tree or two, and then the following spring the slow reparation work would begin, and in two or three years the woods would heal herself, with little lasting damage.

The wide marsh with its salt hay meadows was burned off deliberately every year; that was the way Mr. Quinn fertilized it, or thought he fertilized it. We objected to this process but there was nothing we could do to prevent it, and the marsh always seemed to grow back green over its carpet of ashes before the birds returned. Occasionally someone burned the cattail marsh, although no one was harvesting cattails that we knew of. But that was the way we lost forever our one precious clump of Trailing Arbutus. One summer a fire raced through most of Beech Point, but the beeches and the oaks were too big to be killed by a surface fire, and the undergrowth grew back in the normal way.

We never suspected that arson was a cause of these fires; it was carelessness and plain stupidity, working in an environment of drought. And we never suspected the boy scouts. For all the noise, mess, and minor destruction they caused, the leaving of smoldering fires was not among their sins. They extinguished their fires elaborately and with grave ritual.

The serious fires must have begun during the war years, when we were all scattered across the globe, and our woods were lying unwatched and unguarded. I found myself thinking about them often, at strange times and places. Their verdant mystery, their ageless serenity would come back suddenly and powerfully as I walked down a foreign street in a blackout, as I listened to strange voices singing in unfamiliar woods, and sometimes even in the clangor and cataclysm of battle. Like a cool green island in a world of turmoil, like a haven for the spirit, dreamlike beyond believing, they would be with me. My childhood, my youth, my growing-up, now all but lost. But while I still lived and they lived, I had a vision of the beauty of America to live for.

No one ever discussed the fact during those years that the woods were burning; perhaps no one was aware of it. But now, fires were appearing with disturbing regularity, in almost every season. Sometimes for weeks there would be no sign of fire, and then as if by evil magic another one would flare up, smoulder, burn, and then die or be extinguished. The endemic fires were in evidence, like battle scars on the face of the woodland, when I returned from overseas. For a long time, I could not understand it. Perhaps, I thought, it was the soldiers who came and camped here from time to time, in some form of military training. For months after my return—long after the war was ended—one would suddenly find the woods invaded by platoons of fatigue-

# Fire

uniformed young men (by now there were men younger than I), clutching rifles, moving down our trails, making less noise than the boy scouts but more noise than any infantrymen who wanted to stay alive in combat. They pitched their camp in Warblers Saplings, now a ruined shell, stayed a few days, blew many bugle calls, and then were gone, adding little to the woods' history but much to its buried archaeology. But how could the fires be attributed to the soldiers, when they often seemed to spring up spontaneously, sometimes long after even the echoes of the bugle calls had died? Or could it be the work of some persistent madman with a consuming rage against these acres, who came stealthily at night and struck his match against the tinder of the ground and fanned the flames until the fire was set and steady, and then crept away appeased?

The answer came slowly; the mystery should have been solved with less speculative fantasy and greater attention to the clues. No madman was setting these fires. No soldiers were responsible. The campers and the casual visitors were not the culprits. Not even the sparks from the chimney stack could now be blamed. No one was setting these latest fires. The woods themselves were on fire, and had been for months and years, *beneath the surface of the ground!*

Though we did not know it, and could not see it, somehow during those war years the black muck of the woods had been slowly drying out. Whether it was a series of drought years, or a lowering of the water table through increased pumping (which the water company denied) the truth was that the woods was far less often the water-soaked reservoir it had always been before. True, the Thrush Woods and the Green Cathedral still collected pools of standing water every winter and spring, and the cattail marshes and other low places served as natural basins. But up on higher ground (higher often by merely a foot or two), north of Teal Stream, and around the cattail marsh, the earth must have been drying out. And when it dried, it assumed its true identity which was not soil, not even muck, but peat. This former depression in the land was in reality underlaid by a peat bog, centuries old—an accumulation of humus now compressed but still several feet in thickness—that would fuel an underground fire that might burn on for years.

The underground fire in the Lord's Woods did indeed burn on for years, like a fever, like a malaria that might lie invisible and dormant for months or weeks. Now to disappear underground without a trace, when the surface earth was soaked, lurking in some dry pocket of peat, feeding quietly without a trace. Now to give notice of its presence with wraithlike wisps of smoke that seeped out of the ground, leaking through the moss and ground cover around a tree. Then suddenly a breakout would be visible, with the ground tinder burning to a fine white ash, like an enormous abscess, and little flames licking the exposed roots of the tree. Then for days afterward a slow-consuming fire that would eat and char the roots of the tree and kill it, eventually leaving it to topple to the ground. Then often the fire would suddenly die down and disappear, only to appear again, a month or three months later, fifty or a hundred yards away. Now when we walked through the woods and saw shreds of smoke blowing through the green underbrush, sometimes from more than one place at once, we were filled with foreboding. Perhaps this indeed was the intimation of doom. Here and there throughout the woods were the rootless victims of the fire, some standing in ashy pits, some fallen where the malignancy had struck and then moved on. Would this be how our world ended, in a thin haze of blue smoke rising, and a slow thunder of dead trees?

# EIGHTEEN

# Boom

IT WAS NOT FIRE that destroyed the Lord's Woods. Fire and storm, blizzard and drought, even hurricane and flood were all natural events in the woods' long history, often experienced and always somehow survived, their wounds slowly self-healing and finally obliterated in forgiving beauty. Before the final act could be staged and the curtain rung down at last on the drama that had been unfolding here for thousands of years, there had to appear on stage the villain of the piece—modern man—and there had to be a motive. It was not fire or storm that came to destroy our woods. It was greed and duplicity, avarice and ignorance and apathy.

He came first along Peninsula Boulevard and in those neglected streets we called the Lord Estate (west of the Lord's Woods) soon after the ending of the war. Where long there had been one house or two tucked along a leafy lane, now suddenly there was a row, crowded picture window to picture window; three, four, six, ten. When you walked with apprehension down Longacre or Howard or Derby avenues and through the tall oaks back of Heller's all was clamor and destruction. The contractors had moved in like an occupying army; truckloads of lumber and brick and pipe and concrete blocks lay about waiting to be pieced together. Along the boulevard, signs sprouted, pointing to elegantly named model homes: the Dorchester, the Mayfair, the Park Lane. On the weekends young couples with their parents and a child or two in tow disgorged from their cars to peer into closets and admire the raised dining area with the wrought-iron railing. Almost every week new ground was invaded, the trees and shrubs bowled over, the tangles of blackberry and grape rooted out and obliterated. The value of the land was soaring; those gullible dreamers who had succumbed to the spell of the auctioneer twenty years earlier, those who had somehow hung on, could now get their money back, or even more. It was a miracle!

Now all those grassy lanes we roamed as youngsters chasing the Meadow Fritillary and the Spicebush Swallowtail through canyons of wildflowers tall as we were were widened and paved and lighted, and assumed the banal conformity of suburbia. Some of the builders had left the taller trees to shade otherwise bare plots, but the red maples soon died off, smothered by the sandy fill, the asphalt driveways, and the lowered water table. If the new owners wanted shade they had to plant their own trees, first paying to have the dead monuments removed.

The building and spacing of these new houses were crimes of avarice. Many were built on marshy land that produced flooded basements every spring. The houses almost touched each other, with handerchief-sized gardens and driveways for front lawns. But the new owners had lived all their lives in apartment houses. They judged a dwelling by its interior amenities: the number and size of the rooms, the closets, the work-saving features like the garbage disposal unit, the musical door chimes, and the real wood-burning fireplace. Of course, their first glimpse was a shock—that cleverly distorted rendering in the ad made the little Cape Cod box look enormous, under towering trees and so beautifully landscaped, and here it stood under the hot sun, with its sad little row of arborvitae and laurel "landscaping" and the bare front lawn from which, soon, would sprout thirty varieties of hardy weeds and the builder's tender rye grass, in that order.

The Lord Estate soon disappeared. With it went the abandoned golf course. Almost overnight an entire community blossomed on those meadowland acres. Here were more expensive houses set in spacious gardens. But they too were barely above sea level, for the marsh rimmed their northern border. North of the woods along the Old Gray Road (Rosedale Road was its official name) the farms were disappearing fast. This was not the work of small random developers, as in the Lord Estate. These fertile fields were acquired in vast tracts. Grids of roads were slashed across them and the houses went up blocks at a time, more densely crowded, more monotonously uniform than anywhere around. Whatever modest zoning restrictions had been applied to other environs of the woods had been forgotten here. I looked upon them as rural, ready-made slums, quickly and badly thrown together, and were convinced that they would stand empty as monuments to man's cupidity for years; they were sold and occupied as fast as they were built. No more the crying Killdeer in these fields, no more sweet song at evening from the Vesper Sparrow, or noonday sizzling of the Grasshopper Sparrow. This was a sorry wasteland now, with no single inhabitant of any of those tacky boxes who could remember what had once been here: the corn, the rows of lettuce, the potatoes, the bluestem grass. None could remember a horse and buggy shooting up banners of yellow dust as it raced along, one summer's morning years ago.

The Lord's Woods were at bay. Hordes of people were moving outward into all the suburban counties, lured by the broad new highways that were both stimulating and serving the home building, lured by the prospect of better schools, cleaner air, and a green and tranquil environment. No one could blame them. It was a time of booming economy. Bewitched by the advertising and beset by the American imperative for self-betterment, the young families fled the squalor of the cities to the "rich, full life of the suburbs." It might strain the budget for a time, but Donald was getting ahead in business and the equity in the house would grow (but not as fast as the taxes). So they made that down payment on the little split-level colonial ranch on Bryant or Church or Hungry Harbor Road, which was the fancy name for that dusty track that once wound past the little red farmhouse with the enormous spruce tree, now both long gone, and with the blotchy-faced man and his dogs, all dead and gone.

In those years—the late forties and the fifties—the face of our world changed completely. What had been sleepy semirural villages, each separated from the others by an interval of woodlands or farms and meadows, slowly spread out and merged with one another, until the entire south shore of Long Island was one suburban continuum. The narrow country roads that connected these villages became choked with traffic. Some of the major roads were widened, but new homes and shopping plazas were developed even faster, nullifying the benefit, and going anywhere by car became an agonizing stop-start-stop crawl. Traffic lights proliferated.

Down along the bay road where Anne had first smiled sunbeams at me, all those flower-strewn meadows and the emerald sward of polo field were now bedecked with ornate excrescences, with sweeping driveways and pillared porticos, exuding ostentation in the latest mode. The older streets of the village could change but little, but the few remaining vacant plots added a house or two, and some of the larger properties were subdivided for five or ten or twenty homes. Older houses with smaller gardens, like ours, were coming into new ownership, succumbing to the prices forced upward by the insatiable demand. One by one they were changing hands, and the new owners were busily bringing them up-to-date, transforming old screen porches into playrooms, adding new patios, with here and there a swimming pool or (very posh) a Japanese pebble garden.

With this tremendous surge of immigration and building, the woods stood ever more isolated, an island of wilderness in a sea of rampant suburbia. In all that south shore landscape, this was the only remnant of wet woodland left, the only place where one could lose himself from the frenetic world and be an Indian brave or a Thoreau, a Daniel Boone or a John James Audubon, or just oneself, a child learning about the world around him. Here, relic and reminder, was Long Island as it had been before the first

# Boom

World War, before even the first colonist. How long could it stand against the pressures bearing in upon it from all sides?

The first clue came soon enough, when it was announced that the water company had sold some acreage at the south end. Before we knew it there were pipe lines across the meadows pumping sand, engulfing all that woodland from the Range westward, as well as a chunk of the marsh to the north. Now where there had been darkness and light-flecked mystery under the red maples, all was glaring white sand, alien and lifeless. Left to settle and be leveled, then staked out for streets, utilities, and houses. Boxlike houses were even popping up in that godforsaken strip between the boulevard and the power lines. So great was the demand that even these were bought quickly at high prices, despite the menacing towers and high tension wires that hung directly overhead, in spite of the roaring traffic of the boulevard.

Now all those Jewelweed Woods at the woods' entrance, on both sides of the bow in the Cinder Road, and all the Range itself were obliterated. Where the Range had been, where our arrow slew the squirrel, where Anne's Tree had spread its mantle over us in benison, where the herons roosted and the blueberry and sassafras grew in fields of bracken, where the fox tracks spelled out wonder across the pristine snow, where towhees called and catbird answered was now conquered and annexed, a mere extension now of everyday, another corner of the commonplace.

I found it almost unbearable to come this way any longer, to see what was here and remember what had been, and so I moved away. Only a few miles to the east, but far enough to help me avoid passing and repassing this travesty, with its burden of images and its release of anguish. When, unavoidably, I found myself passing what was left of the Lord's Woods, I would deliberately avert my eyes, telling myself that nothing had changed, that it was still alive, as in my mind it lived, unchanged. It was puerile and unreasoning, but it helped to keep the woods unspoiled in their last refuge on earth: in my heart.

The woods were still there, besieged and battered—at least the inner sanctuary. If you flew into the immense new airport that had annihilated all those miles of marshland we had roamed for years—the Old Mill, the Idlewild Golf Course, the hidden creeks and bays west of the turnpike—you looked down and saw just before landing, an unbroken canopy of forest that was the Lord's Woods, a dark green preserve, geometrical in shape, an anomaly, hemmed in by highways and by rows of boxes. But it was still there. The cattail marsh, the Thrush Woods, the Green Cathedral, the Cinder Road, the Deep Ditch, Beech Point, Stepping Stone Island, Three Bridges, Teal Stream—still there in spite of storm and fire, vandalism and power line, progress and highway, population explosion and home development. One emerald gem shining in all that clutter.

And then the distant, unknown owner moved to doom it.

# NINETEEN

# The Threat

IT WAS CONDUCTED in the deepest secrecy. No For Sale signs ever sprouted around the littered boundaries; no advertisements ever appeared. Through the years many approaches had been made by eager developers, but all had been refused.

But in December, 1955, serious negotiations were begun between the water company and agents for a developer syndicate. No word was ever leaked, and it was months before the first rumors spread in the community, by which time the intricate details of the transaction had been worked out and the deal all but consummated.

For years, we who had been educated, inspired, and enriched in these green precincts had talked wishfully of preserving them forever. How wonderful it would be to turn this besieged woodland and the marsh too into a protected area dedicated to beauty. We discussed the alternatives: an appeal to the absentee owner to declare it a sanctuary on his own, or to deed the land to the community; purchase by an organization or individual dedicated to conservation; or as a last resort acquisition by a governmental agency and dedication as a wildlife area for town, county, or state. We felt a growing sense of urgency, but we did nothing. Dave's Boys were scattered, but the woods remained, slowly deteriorating, but beautiful still, flinging her green skirts each spring over the new litter, still pulsing with the songs of tree frogs on summer nights and the rustle of hidden wings in autumn thickets. That this should ever end was unthinkable. We believed too that the water company was now reduced to its minimum acreage. Where would the millions of gallons needed daily come from if the streams were encased in concrete culverts and the spongy woodland buried under asphalt and gravel?

School District 14 was interested in the woods too, but not for preservation. Anticipating classroom needs five years hence, the school board had approached the water company more than once, vainly seeking an option on some of the acreage, but not yet in desperation. The board believed that it would be notified prior to any sale, and it had available to it the right of eminent domain, claiming a higher public interest than mere home-building. The school board was content to wait and let the land grow more and more expensive.

There had been, nine years earlier, a brief and abortive attempt to obtain from the company, without purchase, the use of the woods for a community conservation education area. The moving spirit behind this campaign had been one Mrs. Roland Bergh, a long-time resident of the area, a worker for conservation, and a passionate devotee of the Lord's Woods.

Helen Bergh's campaign was unsuccessful, but it brought together on the same field of battle many of the combatants who would play important roles in the suspenseful drama of the woods' survival ten years later. She was an advocate to be reckoned with. With an inconsequential "power base," as chairman of the Conservation Committee of her garden club, she could coerce no one. But she was on friendly terms with the county political establishment, which was all-powerful. And she was indomitable.

On March 9, 1946, she called a meeting at which representatives from several interested groups were present. Ways of saving the woods were discussed, and it was agreed to seek advice from the National Audubon Society. Shortly thereafter, with the woods still wintry and bare, Richard Pough, the society's conservation director, came out to explore. On April 10 he submitted his report. "I was most favorably impressed," he wrote. His report listed ways in which the site could be utilized without alterations to the environment, means by which a nature study center could be organized and sponsored, and concluded with seventeen projects which could be conducted there by local school systems and the community at large.

Armed with the report, Mrs Bergh called a second meeting, at which the water company's attorney, Louis Delafield, was present. He was a neighbor and friend of Mrs. Bergh's, and his immediate reaction was favorable. He thought the company would probably have no objection to community use of the woods, but would require full details including a map showing access, parking, proposed trails, nature shed, fencing, and other facilities. But it wouldn't want to deal with a nameless *ad hoc* committee. It would want commitments from some substantial sponsor, such as the National Audubon Society.

Helen Bergh next met with John H. Baker, president of that society, and learned that Baker would be willing to undertake direction of the project, if assured an annual financing of $5,000, and also if responsibility for this were assumed by a single sponsor, such as the Bird Club of Long Island.

But the Bird Club of Long Island balked. The club, founded many years earlier by Theodore Roosevelt and friends, had its own pet project, the Roosevelt Bird Sanctuary at Oyster Bay, and it was not eager to lose its independence in a joint endeavor with the Audubon people. It asked for a year's delay, to "think things over." Undaunted, Helen Bergh then sought sponsorship from local organizations. The Community Chest agreed to make an annual contribution. School District 14 could allocate funds for outdoor education, if the project director could guarantee a certain number of hours to student instruction. The local private schools would help pay the director's salary. The boy scouts would finance the nature museum. And the girl scouts needed an overnight campsite.

But just when all the pieces seemed ready to fall into place, Mrs. Bergh received a formal letter of rejection from the water company, expressing fears that if the company voluntarily re-

# The Lord's Woods

linquished certain property rights, its full title might somehow be jeopardized. The offer was therefore withdrawn.

In her reply, a crushed Helen Bergh asked that if the time ever came when the company wished to dispose of all or part of the property she be notified, since the community was clearly interested in establishing a nature center there, and means might be found eventually to acquire it. This the absentee owner agreed to do.

So it stood for a few years, with the lovers of the woods lulled and waiting, and the slow deterioration of the property continuing. A howling banshee of a storm on Thanksgiving Day, 1950, roared across the land, leaving another havoc of blowdowns and wrenched-off limbs, almost as devastating as a hurricane. What the winds left the underground fire crept like a cancer to consume.

But behind the scenes at the water company all was not somnolence. It did not take much acumen to see the undeveloped acreage disappearing from the surrounding communities with incredible rapidity, and the price of what remained climbing ever higher, with the company's taxes keeping pace. So the company studied its water resources, made predictions of future demand, and arrived at a fateful decision. If it dug new and deeper wells into the Magothy sand layer about 450 feet down and clustered them around the pump house, it could shut down its more distant wells, especially the long south line that ran under the Grassy Road. It could thus still maintain a daily potential of twelve million, against a predicted demand of eight million. With that decision, the fate of the woods was sealed.

The first big chunk to be sold was all that woodland and salt marsh farthest from the pump house, west of the Range. Seventy-two precious acres, and with them the Indian Tree, the pond of the snapping turtle, and Jewelweed Woods. It was 1951, and the new houses were filled with people in 1952. That same year the company began the modernization that included the consolidation of its wells. No more hopper cars of soft coal on the trestle. No more huge steam-driven triple-expansion engines to turn the enormous flywheels of the pumps. The galley slaves who had stoked

the furnaces for three generations were transformed into me-
chanics. The big pump room with its tall windows was dismantled
and partitioned into workshops, engine rooms, control room,
and offices. The windows were bricked in, the smoky, red-brick
exterior painted a somber buff, and the idle smokestacks removed.
The only sound from the pump house now was the endless hum
of diesel motors. All was new, efficient, and ready for the *coup
de grâce*.

And so it came to 1955, with offers having been made and
refused, and then the prospective purchasers agreed upon, late
in the year. For the next ten months, in secrecy, details of the sale
were negotiated, the attorneys for both parties working their
cautious ways through a maze of ancient deeds, with boundaries
and access and easements, some with landmarks long since
vanished. ". . . at that certain parcel of woodland situated on
the north side of Rockaway Neck in the Town of Hempstead,
County of Nassau, bounded beginning at the southeast corner by
a certain stake, running due north by a row of stakes (and woodland of D. T. Jennings) until it comes to a certain brook; then
west down said brook until it comes to a certain ditch . . ."
With some easements that ran with the land ". . . with a privilege
of a bar or gate to cart to and from the woodland . . ." With
zoning ordinances, surveys, and matters of title to be determined.
But the work went steadily forward.

It was a curious business. The promise to Mrs. Bergh had been
ignored. Community interest was never considered. The possibility that the company might get a better price for its land if all
interested parties bid for the prize never seemed to have figured
in company considerations. It was a closely held private company,
and there would be no disgruntled shareholders to mollify. It
was even more curious than it appeared, for the absentee owner
turned out to be a well-known philanthropist, perhaps even a
conservationist, himself. J. Stewart Mott, a director of General
Motors Corporation since its founding, had distinguished himself
in his home town of Flint, Michigan, by a series of munificent
gifts. He had never taken any profits from his little water company. Even the proceeds of the land sale had been earmarked for

plant improvements. Why then this urgency to commit these unique acres to certain destruction?

All during the Winter of 1956 rumors flew that the land was up for sale at last, and the woods lovers bestirred themselves anew. It was Helen Bergh who stirred first, with a letter to Edwin V. Larkin, Presiding Supervisor of the Town of Hempstead, in which the woods and surrounding villages were located. She asked for an interview to discuss alternatives to the threatened destruction. Later in the month the meeting was held, at which the supervisor informed Mrs. Bergh that unless there was immediate and overwhelming public demand for preservation, the Town would do nothing to prevent the development of the woods.

The opening gun of a battle that was to be long and bitter was sounded in a local weekly, the *Nassau Herald*, on May 13. The headline above the brief story read WANT WATER COMPANY PROPERTY MADE PARK. It reported on a meeting earlier that week of the Woodmere-Hewlett Exchange Club, a businessmen's luncheon club, at which a decision was made to start a campaign to save the woods. What the story didn't reveal was that an option/purchase agreement had already been signed, covering 118 acres, between the company and the prospective purchaser and that the company considered the land, "for all practical purposes . . . sold."

Overnight, the fate of the Lord's Woods, now commonly and henceforth called Woodmere Woods, became a topic of local excitement, and for the first time many of those who lived near the woods learned that they had a treasure in their midst and that this jewel was in danger.

On June 5, more than one hundred representatives of various civic groups and other interested persons attended a meeting at the high school, called by the Exchange Club, to consider the future of the water company property. For the first time the conservationists realized the scope of their task. Local opinion was as diverse as it was uninformed; it was not yet sold on the idea of a nature preserve, in spite of ardent presentations by Helen Bergh and Ben Berliner, the only remaining resident member of the Bird Club. Others no less fervent wanted a park, but with mass recreation facilities: playgrounds, baseball diamonds, tennis courts, and picnic grounds. Other factions favored the development of the area for light industry, holding that only this solution could help lower the soaring tax rate for homeowners. Others (more recent arrivals?) would let the developer proceed; homes and neat gardens were more desirable neighbors than thickets of poison ivy and "rat-infested" woodlands "where rapists can hide." The school board, knowing what kind of growth families brought, wanted part of the property reserved for future expansion.

One day after the meeting Helen Bergh addressed a polite, persuasive letter to the absentee owner, recalling his promise of ten years earlier, citing the singular and irreplaceable value of his woodland, and asking that this land be not "immediately sold for housing development, but that time be given for a citizens' group to arrange for its purchase or acquisition." A few days later she received from the owner's son, Harding Mott, a copy of a letter written by W. Victor Weir, the water company president, which stated that there had not been any community interest shown until recently in community use of the seventy-two acres sold in 1951, or in the remaining land. The land itself had been sold and was no longer under the control of the Long Island Water Corporation. It was all very corporate and very correct.

Mrs. Bergh was quick to remind the owner's son of the community concern for the property dating from 1946, that further inquiry had been made six years later, at which time she had been assured that the entire property must be retained for the protection of the wells. But nothing further came of the correspondence.

In mid-June the Exchange Club appointed a fact-finding committee to investigate and evaluate possible alternatives for the property. Early in August, at a meeting attended by people representing the entire spectrum of community interests, the committee reported to the club. All agreed that the best interests of the community would not be served by a housing development in the Woodmere Woods. The usefulness of the woods as a flood control area was cited, and the great cost of a new storm drain sytem to replace this natural safety valve was emphasized. It was a pragmatic and imaginative approach, demonstrating some awareness that, at that time and place, you could not sell beauty and bird song to politicians. With solid community support behind him, the club's president asked for a meeting with the County Board of Supervisors.

Now, with members of the fact-finding committee as nucleus, a new organization was formed—the Woodmere Woods Conservation Committee. The cochairmen were Ben Berliner and Helen Bergh. During the rest of the summer of 1956, and into the early autumn, meetings were held at the Berliner or Bergh house, battle plans were argued and adopted. Funds had to be raised. Legal advice obtained. Public opinion had to be mustered and focused purposefully. Public officials had to be tracked down, cornered (some of them proved slippery), begged, cajoled, and bargained with. Every possible alternative to destruction had to be examined. And there was no time.

No matter how actively the Woodmere Woods Conservation Committee was organizing and mustering public opinion, it was doing nothing practical to delay the sale of the property. On November 8, the other local weekly, the *South Shore Record*, reported that the contract had been signed and the woods sold for $12,000 per acre to a group of investors known as Edgerton Associates, whose only known address was the office of its attorney, Joseph F. Carlino, of Long Beach.

School District 14 was now aroused. A public meeting, called by its Citizens' Committee for November 13, was attended by more than three hundred persons and marked the beginning of community-wide action. Alternatives had been explored by subcommittees prior to the meeting, and their reports were given. Could the Long Island State Park Commission, bossed by the formidable Robert Moses, condemn and purchase the property for a state park? It could, but it wouldn't. Wet woodlands in a remote corner of the county was not Moses' concept of ideal state park land. Would Nassau County itself purchase the property for a combined recreation and wildlife area? No, there was no county-wide demand for such a facility; furthermore it would serve only the neighboring residents and thus be an unjustified burden on more distant taxpayers. The Town of Hempstead was of the same opinion, but suggested that a local park district might be established, if it were supported entirely by the adjacent communities. The consensus of the meeting was that the land should be left in its natural state, fenced, attended by wardens, and locked after dark. Ben Berliner reminded everyone that this was the last remaining woodland in southwestern Long Island and that its loss could not be allowed.

The park advocates now at least knew the identity of their opposition. Joseph Carlino, whose law firm had negotiated the contract, was a man to be reckoned with in Nassau County. An able lawyer and rising figure in state politics, he had first been elected to the legislature in 1944 and re-elected every two years since, had won his spurs on various committees, and finally, two years earlier, had been appointed Assembly Majority Leader, a position of power and trust, reflecting both his own ability and the influence of the county party chairman, J. Russel Sprague. Carlino had become Sprague's protégé in Albany and his second-in-command in Nassau County. The party itself, having enjoyed a half-century of unthreatened control in Nassau County was at that moment enjoying a golden hour of confidence, having only a few days earlier delivered the county to President Eisenhower by a seventy per cent plurality.

It was obvious the party power structure would be of little help in promoting any park plan that ran counter to the wishes of Joe Carlino. But the park advocates were hopeful. Helen Bergh was a personal friend and neighbor of Sprague's, and also of Palmer D. Farrington, the local state assemblyman. Sprague, in conversations with Mrs. Bergh, had repeatedly assured her of his personal interest in the park. Some of the park's most ardent proponents were members of the party power structure. Perhaps, in spite of the anomalous position of Joseph Carlino, something could be arranged.

The game was a subtle one. The philosophy of government was expressed by Presiding Supervisor Larkin. "The people can have anything they want if they are willing to pay for it. But prove to me the people want it." To prove that all the people, everywhere, wanted an esoteric amenity like a public wildlife preserve in 1956 was obviously no easy task. And so while there were no public officials who actively supported the cause of preservation, every one of them spoke encouragingly to the protectionists when they came for help. Some of them even gave advice. But the advice they gave, these friendly, smiling politicians, outlined the most difficult of all possible courses, for all along its twisting route were obstacles, and standing at the very end, with the most cordial of smiles, was Joe Carlino.

On November 20, Dr. Michael Santopolo, Superintendent of School District 14, announced at the Exchange Club that he had managed to ferret out the plans for the Lord's Woods. Of the 177 acres remaining, the company would retain the 45 nearest the pump house. The Long Island Lighting Company would purchase 14 acres. The remaining 118 acres would be developed in one of two ways, either of which entailed a shopping plaza, garden apartments, and single-family dwellings in various price ranges. Both plans required changes in existing zoning, but that was deemed no problem. Both plans would obliterate the woods forever.

Meanwhile members of the Woodmere Woods Conservation Committee and other committees were working hard, faced with a deadline on which no date could be set. Preparations were made to circulate petitions and gather signatures of resident taxpayers in the adjacent areas. The petitions supported a park district under the supervision of the Town of Hempstead. Under state law, the district could comprise only unincorporated areas of the town. However, the neighboring villages could use and support the park by vote of their respective village boards.

The proposed plan was a substantial retreat by the conservationists. Commissioner Moses, although uninterested in acquisition, endorsed the park idea wholeheartedly and had even prepared a schematic development plan. Portions would be reserved for baseball fields, tennis courts, multiple-game hard courts, as well as for picnic areas and campgrounds for scouting, while the remainder (about half) would be preserved in its natural state.

# The Threat

The Fact-finding Committee of the Citizens' Committee (of District 14) made its long-awaited report to a large audience at the Ogden School on the evening of December 5. The meeting ran late into the night; many voices clamored to be heard. It was adjourned without arriving at a decision, but the possible alternatives were now clearly outlined.

The following day, the Conservation Committee opened its campaign for public support with an advertisement in the *Nassau Herald:*

## DO WE NEED A PARK?

### OUR COMMUNITY IS DECADES BEHIND AMERICA IN THE DEVELOPMENT OF RECREATION AREAS.

We need adequate ballfields for our children. We need a place for young and old to skate in winter. We need clay tennis courts for people of all ages. We need a playground for little tots. We need a local woods for 1) scouting activities 2) school nature and science clubs 3) garden clubs and those who enjoy the outdoors.

Although the ad clearly endorsed the multiple-use approach, the conversationists had not completely abandoned the idea of a nature preserve for the entire property. Ben Berliner pleaded this solution at every meeting of the committee, and at scores of meetings of civic, school, social, and other organizations throughout the area. This was their last chance to preserve something unique, he pleaded; this preservation would be of priceless value to generations to come.

New rumors were now in the wind. One held that the developers would soon come up with a new plan that would limit the building to three homes per acre; further, that they would donate five acres for a park along Doxey's Brook (Teal Stream). But they could not be located for confirmation.

In mid-December, another meeting was called by the WWCC. The Reverend Leon Kofod, pastor of the First Methodist Church of Woodmere, spoke eloquently in support of the park. He read a letter that he had written to the Hempstead Town Board. "Unless we look ahead, we will discover that we are making the same mistake that has been made in many of our American cities, forgetting that parks and playgrounds are just as essential to good, healthy and happy communities as schools and libraries." It was a plea that would be repeated countless times across America in the next fifteen years. Meanwhile, the Town Board could give the impression that it favored the park proposal, for it could see into the future with far greater clarity than the park advocates and could see no park where the water company property now awaited its fate.

With swelling ranks and growing enthusiasm the conservationists pressed on. Ben Berliner, his voice charged with emotion, clutching a cockscomb of graying hair, exhorted gatherings night after night, painting beauty into the minds of his listeners. "Nobody who ever heard Ben," recalls one witness "ever came away unconvinced. He was marvelous." Helen Bergh devoted her days and evenings pressuring the power structure for help. Roslyn Sloss recruited a solicitor on almost every block and gathered petitions with more than three thousand names on them. Others like Rhoda Newman and Stanley Rabinowitz were busy soliciting funds, and still others were preparing newspaper advertising and mailing cards and fliers to taxpayers. Soon it was difficult to find a civic association, fraternal or social club, business group or church or PTA or garden club that had not heard Ben Berliner or one of the other park spokesmen, and in the end the WWCC had the endorsement of more than seventy of them. Then the largest and most influential of all groups, the Five Towns Community Council, joined the fight. Everywhere in the surrounding communities people wore white lapel buttons with green lettering proclaiming: I WANT TO SAVE WOODMERE WOODS. Surely, the very mass and weight of public support for the park would force the County or the Town to act.

On January 16, 1957, another WWCC appeal appeared in the *Nassau Herald*. It showed an aerial photograph of the woods, the dark crowns of the giant trees making an undulating sea of foliage, with the marshes to the north and west already littered with their rows of boxes. Beneath the picture was a quotation from Ruskin:

> God has lent us the earth for our life. It is a great entail. It belongs as much to those who come after us as to us, and we have no right by anything we do or neglect, to involve them in any unnecessary penalties, or to deprive them of the benefit which is in our power to bequeath.

The following day the water company was heard from. John L. Farley, Secretary-Treasurer, denied rumors that the woods sale had fallen through. He confirmed that the contract had been signed and a deposit made by the purchaser. The ninety-day option would not expire until February 6 and there had been no request for an extension.

On the political front, Helen Bergh now pressed into service another neighbor and friend, Edward S. Bentley, a corporation lawyer who had grown up with Daniel Lord's sons and had known the Lord's Woods for fifty years. Together, they set out to explore the legal procedure that would be required for the Town, or the County, to establish a park. As expected, their appeals to County officials in Mineola, the County Seat, met with no encouragement. Parks were not, simply, its business. Hempstead Town, being closer to the taxpayers, and feeling the groundswell of public interest, gave the conservationists some advice. Presiding Supervisor Larkin advised Mrs. Bergh and Edward Bentley that the only course open at this late date was to offer a bill to the current session of the state legislature, authorizing a permissive referendum among taxpayers of the involved communities, granting the Town permission to create a park district around the water company property and to tax them to support it. There was no assurance, of course, that if presented, the bill would be passed, or if passed, the governor would sign it, or even that if signed and voted on affirmatively by each of the neighboring communities, that the Town Board would ever act on it. It was a path suitably strewn with impossible obstacles and imperatives in time, but it seemed to be the only path through the wilderness. So Edward Bentley sat down to draft the exceed-

ingly complicated referendum bill, to be introduced in the legislature by some friends as yet unpledged. It could not be whipped
up overnight.

In mid-February, park advocates struggled through a howling
blizzard to still another public meeting. A new plan was now
proposed by the School Board's Citizens' Committee: fifty acres
for park, twenty for school needs. Ben Berliner agreed to support
this plan if the referendum bill failed. There was much concern
about the tax burden the new park might impose. Max Kleiner, a
committee member, reflected widely held views when he proclaimed that "the teaching of conservation and nature study is not
the proper problem of the School Board."

The School Board, in the persons of Dr. Santopolo and George
Hewlett, board chairman, reserved decision. Santopolo, originally
an ardent park advocate, was now cooling to the proposal. Later,
he confided his fear that the added tax burden of the park would
harden resistance to new school taxes, and he needed every penny
for schools.

An important milestone was now passed, apparently without
the park advocates getting wind of it. On February 27, at the
Long Beach offices of Joseph Carlino's law firm, the corporation
known as Edgerton Associates, whose vice-president was Louis
Friedman, Carlino's partner, exercised its option to buy the Long
Island Water Corporation's property. Edgerton Associates that
same day and in that same office, resold the property (at no profit,
they reported) to a syndicate headed by Sol W. Aronson of
Brooklyn and Dr. Norman Brody of Rockville Center, who were
described as "Trustees for some investors." In some accounts the
purchase price was reported as $1,250,000, and in others as
$1,415,000, but neither figure was anywhere near the sum that
could have been realized a few years later by public sale. Neither
Brody nor Aronson, it developed, was the moving force behind
the purchase. It was a man named Lawrence Lever, whose name
appeared on no documents on public file.

Whatever the personnel and relationships of the ultimate destroyers (which had now acquired the name Hewlett Gardens, Inc.), they were fully prepared to act with lightning speed once they had clear title to the property. Despite mounting agitation in the surrounding communities and talk of a public referendum, the bulldozers, the chain saws, and the graders were deployed. Early on the morning of February 28, the day after they bought the property, they moved like an invading army into the Lord's Woods. One by one the century-old oaks, maples, tulips, hickories, ashes, and sweet gums crashed to the frozen ground, and the birds and small animals fled in panic. Within the first week, six acres of the Big Woods had been leveled.

Until that day, the fight to save the woods had been almost exclusively a local concern, a peninsular tempest. (The Rockaway peninsula was sometimes called simply the Peninsula, sometimes the Branch, and the five older villages that comprised it the Five Towns.) But now, with contract consummated and the demolition work begun, the story was revealed to a wider audience. The medium was the young, and highly professional, daily newspaper, *Newsday*, that was now blanketing Nassau County with its alert and aggressive coverage. On March 5, more than a year after the battle to save the woods had begun, *Newsday* discovered the Woodmere Woods. There was no mistaking which side the newspaper was on. It was for trees. The story was not treated as spot news, but as a centerfold feature.

The article described the situation generally, told of the plight of Port Washington, doomed to lose rows of magnificent old trees to a street-widening program, and then quoted Ben Berliner: "Last week we were shocked to see bulldozers move in. Five or six acres have already been destroyed, and they're going strong."

In the same edition, *Newsday* began a series of feature stories entitled "Long Island's Troubled Waters," warning that there was a limit to the underground water supply and that with the population of the county trebling since 1930, experts were warning of an impending water crisis; that with the gradual lowering of the water table, reducing the natural underground pressure that held the invasion of sea water at bay, Long Island's shallow wells might run salt (and short) in years ahead, as they had already done in a forty-square-mile area of Brooklyn, all of which had been abandoned. The story went on to even grimmer pictures:

> As Long Island's expansion gorges itself on trees, ugliness is not the only prospect. Long Island can also give itself an economic headache, watersheds are being destroyed every day, and drainage problems automatically grow. Construction of new storm drains may become necessary in the future. . . . A spokesman for the Nassau County Department of Public Works predicted that "the cutting of trees will get worse before it gets better. And that may take fifty years." He said that the disappearance of trees is literally changing the atmosphere on Long Island. Concrete and asphalt reflect heat, whereas soil absorbs the heat and greenery provides shade and oxygen.

But quality of life was of little concern to most people in 1957. Horace Kramer had calculated the added cost of the new development in terms of the burden put on school taxes. But no one was talking about the intangible cost of smog and summer heat, and the deprivation of natural beauty and an oasis of solitude and silence. The Establishment could not afford to listen, not even to its own Department of Public Works. For the soil and foliage ravaged by Hewlett Gardens, Inc., there would never be redress. The delicate balances that had been working in woodland and marsh for a hundred centuries were being permanently obliterated for private profit.

*Newsday* was now locked into the suspense-filled drama of the Woodmere Woods, and while the editorial pages endorsed the principles of conservation and preservation, the business section, real estate section, and its general news pages rang with announcement after proud announcement of the latest shopping center, housing development, industrial park, power station, highway expansion, population growth, property values, and prosperity.

*Newsday* reporter on the story, Stan Hinton, was not one to neglect any facet of the suspense, or the pathos. On March 6, his

194

story reported on the most important face-to-face confrontation yet.

## BULLDOZERS RIP UP TREES
## GROUP BIDS TOWN HALT RUIN

While bulldozers ripped up trees to make way for a new home development, conservationists pleaded with the Hempstead Town Board yesterday to save Woodmere Woods. . . .

But they were told by Presiding Supervisor Edward P. Larkin, "You can't stop the bulldozers." Larkin said he was sympathetic to the development of a park plan, but that the property owner has a right to do what he wanted with his own land. . . .

Ben Berliner handed over to the Town Board petitions signed by twenty-five hundred property owners of the surrounding communities and told the board that his park proposal was backed by seventy local organizations. Edward Larkin was pessimistic. He didn't think there was time to save it. He doubted that the adjacent villages could get together in creating a park district. He indicated that the cost of condemnation might be prohibitive. The meeting was a disaster, but Helen Bergh was undaunted. The next step, clearly, was to finish Edward Bentley's bill, to find someone to introduce it in Albany, and to nurse it through those devious halls to passage. Time was fleeting; the legislature would adjourn the last day of March. But before the bill was sent to Albany, the Village Boards of the five communities involved—Lawrence, Cedarhurst, Woodsburgh, Hewlett, and Hewlett Bay Park—must vote approval in local referendum.

There were only twenty days left to act before the battle was forever lost. Participants in the final days of agony recall them in terms of exhaustion and anxiety, frenzy and hope: telephone calls by the thousands, meetings and pleas with the members of the five village boards, a frantic beating of the bushes for friends in Hempstead, in Mineola, and in Albany. Edward Bentley, immersed in ancient and modern boundaries, polished his bill, for which no sponsor in Albany had yet been signed. The original park area, comprising only the Lord's Woods, was enlarged to encompass the marshland that remained to the west, where the ruins of Musky's boiler home still lay, in order to bring the park closer to the villages of Lawrence and Cedarhurst, whose assessed valuations were needed.

The Village Board of Lawrence was the first to vote its approval, and other village boards would be voting during the week. Approvals were expected from all of them; after all, they merely asked that their taxpayers be given a chance to speak. But Mayor Ernest Elderd of Cedarhurst had publicly denounced the project, and he had been quoted as saying that he was opposed to the park simply because it would raise taxes. Would the Cedarhurst board, the most "political" of all the concerned boards, support its mayor? It always had.

On March 11, too, Ben Berliner announced that the drafting of the bill was almost complete. Advice had been sought from experts in Albany. One of the advisers was George Halleck, attorney for the New York Conservation Council, the most powerful conservation group in the state. Oswald Heck, State Assembly Speaker and an ardent conservationist, was another. Bentley, with few precedents to guide him, had patterned the important tax provisions of the bill after those in a similar bill which had recently created a park district in Great Neck and which was now law.

On Thursday, March 14, the bill was ready, and its backers formally handed it to Larkin's second-in-command, Supervisor John H. McConnell. With the bill delivered, the first of the two conditions would be met; the approval of the village boards was being pressed. On the previous evening, Hewlett Bay Park and Woodsburgh had added their favorable votes. On Thursday, Hewlett Neck became the fourth village to approve. Only Cedarhurst and Hewlett Harbor, an added starter, remained, and their meetings were scheduled for early the following week. Sixteen days remained until the adjournment of the legislature. The demolition of the woods continued.

That weekend Larkin returned to Long Island, and Helen Bergh talked to him about introducing the bill. Larkin suggested that since prompt action was essential, and only Joe Carlino could assure that action, Carlino himself should introduce the bill—a step that Carlino had already agreed to take. It seemed questionable to the park advocates that the Assembly Majority Leader, so deeply involved with the developers, could be a diligent sponsor of this act of legislation, but the bill would certainly get nowhere without his help anyway.

*Newsday*'s story on Monday sent the conservationists' hopes soaring for the first time in months.

## CARLINO PLEDGES TO "PUSH" LATE BILL
## ON 5 TOWNS PARK REFERENDUM

The story quoted Carlino as saying, "We will make every effort despite the small time remaining to push the proposed legislation." During the weekend, meanwhile, Edward Bentley had been required to amend his bill to include another village on the north of the woods, the development had sprawled north of the Old Gray Road all the way across old Curtiss Field. It was now called Green Acres.

Monday night brought bad news. Although Hewlett Harbor, as expected, had approved the referendum, Cedarhurst had rejected it, the trustees backing Mayor Elderd unanimously. Supervisor Larkin promptly warned that the bill must be redrawn to exclude Cedarhurst, or it would be dead.

Helen Bergh flew immediately to Albany and set up a command post in George Halleck's office to nurse the bill through the tortuous corridors of government. The new bill was published on March 20, numbered Int. 4171. No. 4958, and entitled "AN ACT to amend the Nassau County civil divisions act, in relation to the establishment of a park and recreation district in part of the Town of Hempstead." The bill, which ran to twenty-five pages, gave the voters within the district until August 1 to adopt resolutions to include their villages or areas in the park district; if they did not act before December 1 they were automatically excluded. The boundaries established by the bill included properties with current assessed evaluations of $130 million, but approval was needed for only $125 million worth. Cedarhurst could be safely excluded. Finally, the bill was careful to declare that the park proposed was a public one, and therefore the property was subject to the condemnation law of the county.

Almost at once a new problem arose. Majority Leader Carlino, having received the bill from Supervisor Larkin, read it over and informed George Halleck that he could not submit it to the legislature, because there were flaws in it. Halleck demurred, insisting that the bill was adequately written. Carlino was adamant, and he passed the bill along to the Assembly's Floor Legal Department for review. This department reviewed the draft, put its official O.K. on the document, and shot it back to Carlino.

Eyewitnesses to the scene describe Carlino's reaction to legal approval of the bill: "He was furious." He insisted that there were flaws in the bill and that it would have to go back to the Rules Committee. The spectacle of the putative advocate and sponsor of a bill, one who had promised to do everything in his power to rush its passage, insisting against the expert ruling that his own legislation was faulty, was, to use the mildest possible word, curious. Meanwhile, time was racing by. Less than one week remained before adjournment.

Tuesday's *Newsday* was grim and foreboding.

FIVE TOWNS PARK PLAN HEADS TOWARDS DEFEAT

Datelined Mineola, the story reported that the plan appeared doomed for this year, possibly for good. Valley Stream had turned thumbs down on the referendum, the second of the two "political" boards to so act. There was only one slim chance left for the conservationists. Their bill would have to be redrafted to exclude both Cedarhurst and Valley Stream, while maintaining the $125 million assessment minimum. It could be done, but before the legislature could act on it, the revised draft needed the approval of the Nassau County Board of Supervisors. But the next meeting of that board would not be until Monday, April 1—and the legislature was to adjourn on Friday, March 29.

It looked to everyone that the bill—and the park—were dead. But Helen Bergh said, simply, "We're not dead until Friday.

# The Threat

"You'd be surprised to see the aces we've got up our sleeves." It sounded to many as though Helen Bergh was whistling to keep her spirits up, but in fact she did have one or two straws to cling to. One was the obvious fact that no single member of the Establishment—in the villages, in Hempstead, Mineola, or even Albany—wanted to kill the park in full public view, with so many voters throughout the county in such a state of agitation. If the park must be killed in cold blood, then that deed would have to be done by Joseph Carlino himself.

Helen Bergh's other straw was the assurance that there was nothing wrong with the bill. The redrafted version had the legal consent of the Assembly Floor Legal Committee, the Rules Committee, and even the Attorney General's office.

But the patient had almost stopped breathing. *Newsday*'s story on Wednesday was an obituary.

### HOW THE FIVE TOWNS PLAN
### FOR PARK DISTRICT GOT
### LOST IN POLITICAL WOODS

Datelined Albany, the story reviewed the history of the campaign to save the woods and then reported on the last hours of the dying measure.

Assembly Majority Leader Joseph F. Carlino warned that unless the amendment (excluding Cedarhurst and Valley Stream) were rushed to the capital, the legislators could not act on the bill in time to present it to the local municipalities for approval. Carlino said that passage was impossible because the Nassau Board of Supervisors would not meet until after the legislature had adjourned on Friday. Yesterday he pronounced the bill dead because no amendment had been given to him by the park backers. . . .

It wasn't quite dead after all. Somewhere, somehow, Helen Bergh and friends found the solution. Late Wednesday night the Attorney General's office offered the opinion that the bill did not require approval of the local municipalities in order to get legislative action—that the proposed legislation was so worded that local approval was unnecessary. It added, however, that there were provisions that "might offend" the state constitution, but that this possibility need in no way delay passage of the bill as written, since it would be subject to further review and interpretation before the governor signed it into law, or could be tested in the courts thereafter.

On Thursday, suddenly, it seemed the last of the legal obstacles had vanished. The park advocates were jubilant. Surely Joe Carlino had to call for a vote that day.

But that was not the way it was to be. The Attorney General's office might rule that there was no legal hindrance, but the suggestion that there might be technical flaws in the tax provisions (the same provisions that Edward Bentley had lifted from the unchallenged Great Neck law) was all the reason that was needed, if you were running the show.

### FIVE TOWNS PARK BILL
### LAID TO REST AGAIN

Albany—(Friday) The Five Towns Park Bill, which was killed and revived during the past week, was pronounced dead again yesterday.

Resurrected only three days ago by the state attorney general's office, the bill was buried once again by Assembly Majority Leader Joseph F. Carlino. His reasons: portions of it were unconstitutional.

And so, at the last moment, and standing on the shakiest of ground, Joe Carlino was forced to kill the bill himself, the same bill he had promised to push through.

The bill, he ordered, was not to come out of committee. And the fate of the Lord's Woods was sealed.

Was it a flagrant case of conflict of interest, as Carlino's political foes howled, and as later was charged in newspaper stories? No one will say. The events recounted here are all public knowledge, but many of the fascinating ramifications are locked in secrecy. It is undeniable that Carlino's law firm was actively en-

# The Threat

gaged from the beginning in the sale of the water company property. On March 12, Carlino appeared at a hearing in Nassau County to plead for an easing of zoning restrictions to permit Hewlett Gardens, Inc., to build garden apartments and shopping centers on the property, so it is obvious that he was personally involved at the very time he was promising every possible assistance in pushing the park bill through the legislature.

Mr. Carlino has been asked personally and in writing to shed further light on the subject, but he prefers to let the questions go unanswered. At a legislative hearing a few years later which was investigating a different alleged conflict of interest involving Carlino (following which he was given a 174-1 vote of confidence by his peers), the Majority Leader was quoted as saying, in effect, that if conflict of interest should ever become a cause for expulsion from the legislature, and all present conflicts were revealed, the halls of the state legislature would be swept clean.

Horace Kramer quotes Robert Moses in summing up what happened to the Lord's Woods, and Kramer says "you can quote me." Moses had applied the statement to the kind of zoning that was perpetrated on Long Island in 1955. Kramer applies it to the rape of the Lord's Woods, "a collusion between hit-and-run speculators and inept politicians." Kramer, whose participation in the battle to save the woods launched him into politics, sums up his memories of those heroic days. "The Town of Hempstead, particularly in its land areas outside the incorporated villages, provided a field day for speculators (developers), because that's where the big buck was. The developers were required to donate three per cent of their acreage for park purposes, but the Town could take money in lieu of land, and it always took the money. The rule of the fifties was 'cooperate with the real estate speculators'; it was a calculated policy. If the Establishment had in any way been interested (in the five Towns Park District) it would have gone through in five minutes."

For Kramer it was a time of awakening and of shared inspiration. There was Stanley Rabinowitz, who gave his heart, strength, and money out of his pocket, "a fighter, an immortal." Helen Bergh, Ben Berliner, Edward Bentley, Elihu Modlin—countless

201

# The Lord's Woods

others. "We had the finest public-spirited people; I found myself associated with credits and ornaments to the human race."

The death knell of the woods was sounded that day in early spring of 1957, a day when the first vanguard Phoebes were sneezing beside Three Bridges and an early Mourning Cloak or two fluttered on wet wings down the Grassy Road of the abandoned south pipe line. And anyone could hear on the distant perimeter the muffled whine of the chain saws, the clank of bulldozers, and the reverberations of the falling trees.

But even then, somehow, the park advocates kept hoping for a miracle. Was there some unknown benefactor, such as a foundation or a family trust, that might buy, even at an outrageous price, the remaining acres? Was there some new legal approach that might be taken? How about a community college to be located on part of the area, with parkland for the rest? Could not the school board, even at this late date, be induced to change its mind about combining school requirements with park preservation? Again the conservationists pleaded, petitioned, exhorted, and were rebuffed. Only one avenue seemed to offer a glimmer of light: reintroduce the bill, revised to prevent any possibility of attack on legal grounds, and hope to save the still substantial woodland the developer had not yet invaded. Including the marshlands to the westward, there were still almost two hundred acres that could be saved.

On February 25, 1958, State Senator Daniel Albert, of Rockville Center, introduced a "Five Towns Park District" bill into the state senate, and the same day Assemblyman Palmer D. Farrington presented the identical bill to the assembly. Albert's bill called for a park district practically identical to that proposed the previous year, and most of the other provisions were similar.

This time the reaction was swift. By the month's end, a solid phalanx of opposition was ranked against the bill in the county and in Albany. State Controller Arthur Levitt expressed grave doubts about a section of the bill that was angering the mayors: that any deficit incurred by the park district could be made up by a tax on the entire county. That this eventuality was virtually impossible, considering the affluence of the proposed district and its continuing increase in value, was not considered. That the park might be of benefit to a population far beyond the bounds of the district itself was unthinkable. That other parks had been purchased (and would be increasingly acquired) with town and county funds without regard to whether they served neighborhoods or the entire county was not mentioned. Whether the proposed bill was actually unconstitutional, and irreparable, was never determined. The Establishment did not want this particular park, and, for the last time, that was that.

The date of the second and final death blow was March 26, 1958. What was left of the Lord's Woods came crashing down.

For thousands of years there had been wilderness here, pulsing with life, changing subtly and evolving slowly in response to the earth's climate, the geological forces beneath the earth's crust, and in harmony with its own varying fertility. Now all was ended.

One hundred and seventy centuries earlier these same acres, this same pinpoint on the earth's surface, at 40° 38' North Latitude, 73° 47' West Longitude, stood almost in the shadow of a towering rampart of ice, the southern flank of the last glacial advance that had buried the entire northern half of North America, in places almost two miles deep. A polar bear, standing on this windswept, frozen crescent of sand and looking northward might have seen, looming salmon red through the mist, the jagged, columned ice cliffs less than ten miles away, stretching from the southwest across the northern horizon to disappear eastward far across the barren plain.

At the edge of the glacier wall, a dike of earth and rock had been heaped, several hundred feet in height—earth and rock that had been shoved down from the north, like gravel before a bulldozer, and left in rolling ridges. From countless gaps in these ridges and from waterfalls that splashed down from the glacier wall, icy meltwater flowed southward across the sandy plain in a web of interlacing waterways to the sea.

# The Lord's Woods

But the sea in those distant times was nowhere to be seen. Its surface, perhaps three hundred feet lower than today, had receded far to the southward, and what is now Long Island extended out to meet it in a broad, barely sloping outwash plain. This landscape was almost level, spread over with sand and coarse gravels that the braided streams carried with them, punctuated here and there with a hillock or slight rise of ground, but dotted and laced everywhere with pools and ponds and sloughs and bogs and stream beds: shallow, sandy-bottomed streams that flowed with the gray, turbid waters of the melting glacier and the rains.

During the brief chill summer months when the ground was bare, although still frozen solid a few inches below the surface, this featureless landscape harbored a vast assemblage of birds and animals, although it was only a remnant of the hordes that had bred each summer across the roof of the continent before it was ice-buried. But, with all but a few refuges in the far north gone, Long Island was part of the continent's high arctic. Here, at the site of the Lord's Woods, the white wings of arctic gulls flashed across the sky. In the creeks and bogs a gathering of arctic-nesting waterfowl raised their young: eiders and Brant and Old Squaw and scoters and Harlequin and Labrador ducks. Along the stony shores skittered the turnstones and Purple Sandpipers. Here, too, nesting in the sparse grasses that had sprung up in this brief interlude between long winters, were longspurs and Snow Buntings. Preying on them and on the smaller mammals were the jaegers, Snowy Owls and Short-eared Owls, and the Rough-legged Hawk.

The birds did not have the barren ground to themselves. The arctic animals that had moved southward before the advancing ice mantle thousands of years earlier were still here: the great white ice-floe bears, the musk ox, the Barren Ground reindeer, the gray wolf, the arctic hare, and the ermine. In the frigid seas that lapped the island's distant beaches seals and walruses swam, and along those shores, too, surfaced whales: little white whales and the giant blue.

No mammoth bones have ever been found on Long Island,

but a few miles to the north and west the woolly mammoth roamed this same bog-laced landscape, and he was almost surely here too, crossing the wide Hudson River on the winter ice.

Forty centuries pass, the earth has moved through several warmer and colder cycles, and the icy burden which for thousands of years has alternately advanced and retreated across the northern horizon is preparing to leave it for the last time. In July the average temperature is close to fifty degrees and all that remains of the great Wisconsin glacier is a deep-imbedded chunk that fills the river basin to the north of Long Island that will some day be called Long Island Sound.

As the ice vanishes, the land that has been compressed by its weight begins imperceptibly to inch upward again. But the seas are rising still faster as the continental icecaps melt, and Long Island begins to lose, along its southern shore, the sandy slope of the continental shelf that the ice age had exposed. Grain by grain, pebble by pebble, the seas are reclaiming their own.

With the warming of the summer air and the lengthening of the snow-free season, the island swiftly (as geological time is measured) grew for itself a mantle of vegetation. It no longer resembled the barren littoral of today's Baffin Island at the glacier's edge; it was the tundra landscape of the Hudson Bay shore. It was still high arctic, spread in summer with the grays and greens of lichens and reindeer moss, with heaths like Labrador Tea, with andromeda, vacciniums, and a host of arctic flowers. Where the ground was low and wet, in countless little ponds and bogs, the margins were lined with sedges and the plumes of equisetum. Today we would call this oozing ground the muskeg. Living in this vegetation were the littlest animals: shrews and voles and lemmings, and the larger ones, the mink, the marten, the river otter, and the snowshoe hare. The caribou and musk ox still roamed the tundra with the gray wolf and the arctic fox, but among the grasses and the quick-flowering plants nested myriad sandpipers and plovers, waterfowl and ptarmigan. The air was filled again with music—the tinkling of countless redpolls, White-crowned and Savanna Sparrows—the same sweet songs we hear them sing today. No trees yet grew to interrupt the tundra landscape save those prostrate foot-high dwarfs of willow, rhododendron, and spruce.

There can be little doubt that bird and animal life was abundant on the Long Island tundra and perhaps more varied than in the arctic tundra today, for the life-supporting area of the continent had been reduced by half, and all those species which now are spread across the vast reaches of the Canadian and Alaskan arctic were compressed (and greatly reduced in numbers) into a tundra zone no more than one or two hundred miles in depth. Some species indeed must have diminished to perilous numbers, and some disappeared entirely.

We have found no evidence that man was anywhere on the scene in those harsh centuries. Although there were bands of hunting Indians scattered across the continent from California and New Jersey southward into Central America, no trace of man has been found from the early post-glacial period on Long Island. He may have hunted along these shores and taken shellfish from these waters, but the winters were long and frigid and the summers brief, wet, and swarming with insects; this was a bleak and hostile world.

The earth's climate was ameliorating, the oceans were rising, and the glacier had retreated (but with periods of advances and other static periods) across the future Great Lakes and into Canada. The barren zones were far to the northward and the arctic birds had moved northward with them, occupying the ice-edge beaches as soon as they were exposed. The tundra had moved northward across the northern mountains, and Long Island was low arctic. No longer pure tundra, but invaded by scattered stands of forest trees, at first dwarfed and stunted on the higher ground, then gradually full-sized: black spruce, white fir, white pine, oak, willow, birch, and cedar. Park tundra, we would call it today. The time is 9,000 years ago.

For the first time in hundreds of centuries, the site the Lord's Woods was woodland, a dark promontory crescent with a pond at its heart, a pond where sedges and water plants were slowly moving in from the periphery and would in time conquer it,

# The Threat

changing it from pond to bog, from bog to marsh as first we knew it. Our woods were tree-covered, with the streams flowing through them westward to the bay. The woolly mammoth was gone forever but the giant mastodon, last of his kind, roamed the landscape, browsing on the tender shoots of the spruces, firs, pines, and larches. The woods, growing on sand and glacial till were not yet lush and verdant, but in summer they rang to the songs of the Gray-cheeked Thrush, the Blackpoll Warbler, and the White-winged Crossbill. The man we know today only as the Early Hunter may have pursued the mastodon here, as he did all across Europe, but no traces of him have been found. We know that he reached Nova Scotia, which may have had a climate much like Long Island's, as early as 8,600 B.C.

For a period of perhaps twenty centuries the climate turned warm and dry, and the seas continued to advance. Long Island was covered by boreal forest based on a thin, weak, sandy soil. Only in the river valleys and the bogs was a rich fertility developing. The glacier was almost gone, with but remnants far north in Canada. The arctic birds and mammals returned to their ancestral homes, multiplying rapidly to fill the vast breeding grounds open to them. The tundra covered much of northern Canada and south of it marched the dark, dense stands of spruce, pine, tamarack, birch, and fir. Into the hemlock and pine forests of Long Island filtered the first of the broad-leaved hardwoods from the south: oaks and chestnuts, beeches, maples, hickories, ash, and elm. In and out of our woods roamed wolf, bear, fox, wolverine, fisher, and marten. In those open glades moved moose, elk, and deer, and, surely, scattered bands of human beings. Hunters and gatherers only, without bow and arrow, using spears with finely fashioned flint points; perhaps even without fire. They lived primarily on deer, turkey, shellfish, and any nuts and berries they might gather. Long gone were the tundra birds and animals and fast going were the birds of spruce forests—Gray Jays and Northern Shrikes, Hawk Owls, Ravens, and the twittering Boreal Chickadees.

Long Island had assumed its present shape and size and something very like its present climate. The seas had long since invaded the wide valley north of the moraine hills, filling Long Island Sound. The land had ceased to rise from the release of its glacial burden; in fact, it was slowly sinking again, perhaps six inches or less each century. The year was 4,000 B.C. For the next thousand years or so, the woods basked in a warm, moist climate, and then it was dry again. There were only a few relic hemlocks and pines, reminders of bygone boreal ages. The predominant trees were hickory and chestnut, oak and elm. The archaic Indians roamed these acres in greater numbers, setting up their temporary camps, sometimes on high ground above a stream, sometimes along the edge of a tidal creek or bay. Food was abundant and varied; their flint-tipped arrows brought geese and swans and grouse and turkeys. They feasted on bear and deer and moose, beaver, and possibly the firm and tasty flesh of the woodland bison. There were acorns and berries to gather, and huge fat oysters, ten inches or more across, beneath the sparkling bay waters. For centuries these primitive people lived in and out of our woods, in harmony with the world around them, causing nothing but an occasional fire to disturb the delicate balance of their world; never populous enough to take but a minimum of the animals around them or to pollute with their campfires or their spoil, the air and water.

We can find abundant evidence of their presence on Long Island from about 2,200 B.C. onward. All that is left of these silent precursors are the ashes of their open-pit fires, their spear and arrow points, their stone scrapers, firestrikers, axes, and knives. We can see the implements and ornaments they fashioned from bone and shell, and their first stone pots. Much later, from 1,000 B.C. onward, we find them fashioning pottery from clay, smoking pipes, learning cultivation, and beginning to catch and eat fish. By then the Lord's Woods looked much as it did when the first white men saw it. As the centuries moved slowly towards their coming, Indians moved in from the north and west, displacing and exterminating those older natives. These newcomers were Woodland Indians and they called themselves the Reckawecks.

It was in this way, as a green and peaceful Eden, with the

# The Threat

smoke of scattered fire pits drifting across the forest canopy, that the first settlers came upon it. It was a place of lush and rustling beauty, but scarcely of any interest or value, because it was swampy and often flooded, full of mosquitoes and fever. Even the Indians avoided these insect-plagued woods in summer, moving their families, their pots, tools, and weapons to the shores of nearby creeks and bays. There they gathered shellfish from the clear bay waters, paddled their dugout canoes down winding waterways to take with line or net the teeming fish and hunt the abundant waterfowl, while the squaws tended the well-kept farm fields. The corn was planted in even rows, with a fish buried in each hill for fertilizer, and a bean vine trained to wind around the cornstalk. Squash and melons, pumpkins, peanuts, and tobacco were staple crops, cultivated and kept weeded with a hoe fashioned from a Venus clam shell, the soil kept sweet with oyster-shell gravel.

Planting time was traditionally "when the oak leaves were long as a mouse's ear," which was also the time the first wave of migrating warblers danced through the tops of those same oak trees—Myrtles, Black-throated Greens, and Black-and-whites, singing the same songs to the Indians they sing now to us.

In the autumn the Indians moved back into their winter homes in the woods; into the chestnut-bark-covered long houses with their reed-thatched roofs and their row of central fire pits along the line of the ridge, which was open to the sky. For some of the smaller family groups, circular wigwams were preferred. Here in this cluster village the Indians were nearer the hunting and sheltered from the worst of the winter winds. Here too they held the wild religious festivals they called their powwows.

They lived well, in a simple, natural way, these Rockaway Indians, in age-old harmony with the wilderness around them. They were tall, straight, and slim, very quick and graceful in their movements, their bodies anointed with bear grease or eagle grease or fish oil to repel the voracious musketto. Food was abundant and varied: they feasted on fish, shellfish, frogs, and turtles, on game such as turkey, grouse, pigeon, heath hen, geese, and duck; on meats like bear, raccoon, skunk, muskrat, fox, rabbit, and an especial delicacy—beaver tail. Perhaps the staple meat was deer. Cultivated vegetables and wild fruits gathered with nuts, berries, and mushrooms were part of the harvest. Some were stored in pits for the lean winter months, along with the smoked fish, shellfish, and deer meat.

These were Iroquois Indians, who spoke a dialect of the Algonquian language which was common throughout eastern North America. They were a peaceful people, content to stay within the boundaries of their own South Shore–Jamaica Bay focal area, with only an occasional dispute with the neighboring Canarsies to the west or the Merokes to the east. But each year they paid tribute to the more warlike Pequots from the land across Long Island Sound. There is no single spelling of their name (or anything else from those early colonial days); one may find accounts of the Reck-a-wecks, Requia aackies, or Reck quackies. Eventually it became simply Rockaways. Some say the words meant "sandy place," others that it was "lonely place." Now, no one knows.

Footpaths wound between their little villages, marked perhaps here and there with the same bent trees of the kind we found at the bend in the Cinder Road. It was a quiet land; today's Long Islander, his ears outraged and numbed by the roar of street traffic, jet aircraft, power tools, sirens, and all the other noises of our mechanized world, would be struck with the pervading silence of those times. Only the sound of an ax on tree, or wolf-dogs barking, or children playing might intrude on the sounds of bird song and the wind.

For centuries untold these people lived on these lands and waters making no destructive impact on the environment; even those fires they set every spring to burn out the underbrush so that the grass would grow thick for the deer had no permanent effect. They belonged to the woods and were as much a part of it as the turkey, the bear, and the wolf.

Then, in the mid-seventeenth century, the first white settlers came among them, trading coats and knives and bolts of cloth and bushels of grain and getting the best land on the peninsula in return. These were English colonists discontented with New England, moving into the edge of the scattered Dutch villages around the mouth of the Hudson River. They were content at first to occupy little hollows on the high ground along the spine of the peninsula, nestling their tiny houses behind any slight slope that might protect them from the northwest winds of winter. Here they cleared an acre or two of woodland and plowed their home fields, letting their cattle roam the meadows and the marshes. A footpath following the Indian path wound down through the peninsula, joining the farms; eventually it crossed the marshes to the mainland, becoming the famous Rockaway footpath.

The entire peninsula, which was then called the Necke, or the Rockaway Necke, was then, as now, part of the Town of Hempstead, populated by displaced New Englanders, under the rather distant and permissive administration of the Dutch. From the viewpoint of the villagers of Hempstead, the western end of the Necke was far Rockaway, the eastern end, where it joined the mainland, near Rockaway, and from one end to the other, ideal pasture land. One milk cow might be kept in the home lot, but the rest of the family's cattle were driven south in spring onto the Necke. With bays on both sides and a fence across the near end, it made a perfect communal range. Every spring the meadows were burned to encourage the growth of grasses.

By 1647 there were sixty-two freeholder families in Hempstead and most of them kept cattle on the Necke. There was, in those days, perhaps the earliest instance of that hallowed American conflict between rancher and homesteader; the settlers with homes and farm fields on Rockaway Necke forever complaining of the damage done to their crops by the grazing cattle. In the end the homesteaders, as they usually have, won the argument. The official town cowkeeper was required to see that his charges did no damage and was liable if he failed. Freeholders with meadows on the Necke were required to maintain proper fences and gates. One of the earliest recorded cowceepers, or kowceepers, was one George Huylit, Huilet, Huelit, Hewlette, or

# The Lord's Woods

Hewlett, depending on how the Town Clerk wished to spell it. In 1657 he was instructed by the town fathers that as part of his duties:

> hee shall go fourth every morning by that time the Sonn is ½ hower above ye horrison, and not come in before Sonn setting,

> hee is to water the calves twise in ye day at ye leaste,

> hee is to keep yee Calves in ye field 3 weeks and yf any damage be done by his default he is to be responsable.

There was still some trouble from poaching Indians and from the wolves. But the last of the wolves was killed on May 28, 1663, by Henry Disborow, and it brought a 25-shilling bounty. (The bounty to Indians for killing wolves was 2 shillings sixpence.)

There had been a drawing for the land, among the freeholders, in 1647, and another was held in 1659. By then, most of the town lands on the Necke had been alloted. Along with the meadows and the marshes and the broad fertile acres which had been traded for bushels and bolts they now had metes and bounds, were surveyed, fenced, willed, transferred, and sold for pounds, shillings, and pence. The deeds were duly recorded in the Libers of the Town of Hempstead. The Necke was still largely used for pasturage, but slowly new settlers moved in, bought property from the original freeholders, and built little clusters of houses around the crossings of the footpath (now a wagon track)—villages that would someday be the Five Towns.

The Indians were faring badly. As the settlers began to devastate their game with guns, as they gave up their lands and their seasonal mobility, as fever and disease (a smallpox epidemic in 1662 decimated their numbers) and alcohol ravaged them, as they lost their tribal identity and ancestral culture under the impact of the new culture they could neither adopt nor conform to, they degenerated from the masters and inheritors of the land to its derelicts, clinging to the very edge of existence. There had never been very many of them—less than a thousand, perhaps

# The Threat

only a few hundred on this peninsula—and soon there were only
scattered remnants.

Forced back into the marshes and woods, living permanently
along the marshy creeks in miserable shacks and hovels, their
guns taken away by an edict in 1675, some become handymen
and servants; some worked as fishermen, whalers, or on the farms
of the settlers; some peddled from door to door, their backs laden
with fish nets and fishing rods, baskets, sand, vegetables, or bayberry wax. Some were thieves and beggars, poachers or drunk-
ards. By the middle of the eighteenth century there were only a
handful of families left; most of these were only part Indian. The
last of the Rockaways died in 1818, an old man with a fund of
ancient lore and legend. His little house was in Woodmere, where
Linden Street now crosses Broadway, the old footpath. Years
later another old man, who remembered being enthralled with his
stories as a boy, erected a monument to him nearby.

Here lived and died
Culluloo Telewana
A.D. 1818
Last of the Rockaway Iroquois Indians
who was personally known to me in my boyhood
I owning this land have erected this
monument to him and his tribe.
Abraham Hewlett, 1888.

It is the only memorial to a 7,000 year history to be found
anywhere.

Their woods survived a little longer, keeping the traces of
their bent trees and footpaths and camp clearings, but long since
having seen the last of the moose, the woodland bison, the bear,
the Turkey, the Passenger Pigeon, the Heath Hen.

It all happened slowly—so slowly that in no man's lifetime,
save our own, could anyone remember seeing a sudden change,
or any change at all. Year after year the moving seasons advanced
across the woods, transforming them miraculously from brown
and gray to golden green, and then through darker green to
bronze and ochre and orange and russet and then to gray again,

213

# The Lord's Woods

blanketed with white. Year after year, century after century, the woods had continued unspoiled, pristine, unsullied. Until our lifetime. Ours, the earth-defacing, soul-destroying generation.

Now the time of death was come at last. We had watched helpless as the sickness of the twentieth century ate at its heart—the cancer of man-made fire, the infection of man-made litter, the corruption of man-made pollution of its air, its waters, and its silences, the raw incisions of power lines, pipe lines, and highways, the defacements of dump and pipe yard and campgrounds. All these blows it had suffered and might survive. But now the special, final *coup de grâce* of our generation had been struck, and there was no straw left to grasp at. The new glacier had arrived: the dredge with its marsh-destroying sand fill, the developer with his power saws and bulldozers, his asphalt and his concrete, using all the skills of our technology to envelop and obliterate, in the name of holy profit. Finally to accomplish what flood and fire, ice and hail, disease and tempest had not been able to do. Greed and apathy, deceit and arrogance, ignorance and blindness to future needs had finally done their dirty work.

# To Save Our World

THE STORY of the Lord's Woods, its centuries of glory and days of agony, has not been recalled merely as a memorial for an enchanted plot that is gone forever, but also in the hope of salvaging some benefit from its loss.

What invests this brief obituary with such vital import to every American who loves his country as much for its natural beauty as for its gross national product, as much for its havens of peace and harmony as for its conquest of outer space, is that the obliteration of these woods is a classic example of what we have been doing to our beloved America, with terrifying acceleration, for three and a half centuries. With almost no one anywhere, until today, to cry "halt!" or even "shame!" Perhaps each of us has a Lord's Woods of his own, held treasured somewhere deep in his heart, that is now but a fading memory, victim of our pell-mell pursuit of "progress." And for the ones we know and mourn personally, how many thousands of others have fallen without protest to the airport engineeer, the highwayman, the pipe and transmission lines, the box builders, the billboard, and the dump? Year after year we stand helpless as more and more of our heritage is ravaged and despoiled, and the world in which we must spend our days scarred, outraged, and turned hostile.

Today, at last, there are many voices crying "shame!" Environment is the discovery of the decade, and daily the media of mass communication (and the corporate profiteers of destruction too) remind us of their new-found awareness of what we have done to America the once-beautiful. Suddenly we are assailed with sordid pictures and sickening stories of pollution that will some day be cleaned up, and every politician in the land is an instant ecologist. No longer can the embattled taxpayer at the school budget hearing cry out that "environmental education is not a proper subject of public instruction!" Centers for these studies spring up on all sides; recreation and park departments quietly add the words *conservation* or *environmental quality* to their titles. Organizations, private and public, to improve the environment proliferate across the land. No longer is the conservationst publicly branded a bubble-headed enemy of progress, an impractical do-gooder, or simply a bird-watching nut. Now he is called upon by the decision-makers to give expert testimony. But his views are noted with the same polite interest and private scorn as they were twenty years ago, and the decisions made almost never reflect what he has recommended.

The technicians of destruction still command the center of the stage; it is they who have the unassailable statistics and are on the side of the unassailable progress. The legislators and the administrators need and accept their financial support and are quick to do their bidding. The airport, after all, must expand somewhere, the highway must add four lanes, the power plant must go into the park, the pipe line across the tundra, the factories into the marsh. Banning billboards along our scenic highways is a splendid idea and so we pass a National Highways Beautification Act. But the billboards somehow remain; there's too much private profit involved. The governmental commissions and agencies that make the decisions and carry out the laws are packed with partisans; often they are former executives of the very companies they must regulate, and their decisions are predictable.

For all the new awareness and the millions of aroused citizens who are becoming involved, America is still losing the environmental war on a thousand battle fronts, while making much of our pitifully few victories. For every scrap of wetland or wood lot that someone manages to snatch from the jaws of ticky-tack, a thousand virgin acres fall to the combined pressures of population and profit. We are buoyed by our little victories, and deluded. For our forces have been spread so thin; they are facing forces so powerful, that as we bar one door, they come through a hundred windows. We are learning how to make it more difficult for the enemy to achieve his victories: how to delay him in the courts and how to mount public indignation against him. But in the end, he almost always wins.

You can fight the exhausting fight to save one patch of woodland here, or a corner of wetland there, but even when you win, the victory is ephemeral. While you are celebrating victory here, they are rushing through four more disastrous projects elsewhere. How do you argue against them? How can you compare the values of green foliage and green grass and serenity against the imperatives of progress? How do you measure the needs of the small boy collecting tadpoles in a jelly jar against the demands of a metropolitan transit commission?

But he is not just one small boy. He is all of us. He is generations of Americans who deserve the right to live in an America where there is beauty and harmony and even wilderness within reach of him and school and even his bedroom window; a Grassy Road to lalligag along on a spring morning, a Jewelweed Woods to burst through on an October afternoon, a Three Bridges to lie down upon over flowing water on a lazy summer noon, and a Green Cathedral to waken him to the total integration and utter interdependence of all life on earth, including his own. The Lord's Woods was not just a playground for Dave's Boys. It was a schoolroom, a microcosm of the world, a living textbook of life and history and art and beauty and the art of living and growing up responsible. It was our America, and it taught us reverence. We cannot lose our Lord's Woods, wherever they remain. We must save them to save our souls and the future of America. With all our strength and dedication, and with every tool of public education and private persuasion we can muster, we must now cry "halt!" to the rape of America.

It is not the purpose of this book to add to the growing

literature on the "how to" of environmental protection. There are excellent texts now available, and new titles appear almost daily. The interested citizen can begin to find on the shelves of his local library useful books and scores of pamphlets on pollution, ecology, and related subjects. William H. Whyte's *The American Landscape* and *Challenge of the Land* and Ian McKarg's *Design with Nature* should be in the hands and minds of every private and governmental executive responsible for planning, zoning, and construction. There are too a host of national organizations joining the common cause. The Environmental Defense Fund has demonstrated how the citizen can use the courts to fight pollution. The Open Spaces Action Institute, the Nature Conservancy, America the Beautiful Fund, the Sierra Club, the National Audubon Society, and countless other national organizations are dedicated to the preservation of the best that is left of America, and each exhibits a slightly different area of concern. They are helping and need our help.

But they cannot do it all. Environmental quality cannot be a way of life in America until it becomes a deeply felt, universal hunger, as strong as the hunger for progress and profit. And this will never happen unless and until the people who feel the devastation most keenly and see the dread future most clearly commit themselves personally to the cause. Not merely by sending their dues to the National Wildlife Federation or to the Ad Hoc Committee to Save Stump Pond. Not just by attending angry meetings of the Sportsman's Council or the Ladies' Garden Club. But by direct, personal political action.

By this we mean active involvement in every level of the political process from the precinct and the election district to the village, town, city, county, and state. By whatever means available: by volunteering first for menial service, by working for the nomination and election of fearless and declared conservationists, by helping to formulate goals and platforms, and by running as candidates themselves. One bird watcher on the Village Board of Selectmen, one conservationist on the Town Recreation and Parks Commission, one ecologist in the state legislature is worth a thousand passionate letters to the editor. One Franklin Roosevelt in the White House, or a Stewart Udall as Secretary of the Interior, is worth ten million signatures on petitions. The corporation lawyers, the agents of big business, the technicians of destruction, the career politicians have had our government to themselves far too long. We have seen how they joined forces with the profiteers of blind despotic "progress," and at what dreadful cost. Now it is time to cry "halt!" Are we less qualified than they to set the course that America must follow to save itself from total degradation? Do we have a less valid vision than they of what America can be?

The advance legions are already at work. The young people of America are with us. There is no lack of potential leaders among us. It is we who can lead America out of her long sleeping sickness, the sickness that killed the Lord's Woods and millions of other precious acres of America needlessly, and into the bright world we know is possible.

# THE
# LORD'S WOODS

### A reconstruction
### of their state about 1930

Robert Arbib
Richard Edes Harrison

dump

Little Red
House

OLD GRAY ROAD

N.J.

BRONX

N

MANHATTAN

QUEENS

NASSAU

BROOKLYN

J.F.K.

Valley Stream

Hewlett
Woodmere

Cedarhurst

Lawrence

S.I.

Rockaway Peninsula

Long Beach

0   1   2   3

miles

ditches

salt marshes
(spartina grass)

Mo

salt m

Teal Str

pampas

Thr

Anne's
tree

Willows

Jewelweed

The Range

Turtle
Pond

Indian
Tree

Wood

bar

Cinder Road

PENINSULA

Golf course

orchard

FUTURE

Owl Tree

Quinn Farm

## KEY

woodland

grass

streams

major trails

future
construction

ROAD

WESTWOOD

Woodmere

Academy

Map of the Lord's Woods by Richard Edes Harrison